THE FIRST VOYAGE

BILL ARMSTRONG

DEDICATION

I wish to dedicate this Book to all my Shipmates that were Crewmembers aboard the USS Chincoteague, AVP-24, during the month of July, 1943 and to those Shipmates, who made the ultimate sacrifice on July 16, 1943. Their lives will forever be remembered on the Memorial Wall of Remembrance at the Nimitz Museum of the Pacific War in Fredericksburg, TX

**This Plaque Dedicated to
all who served aboard this vessel during WW II
April 12, 1943 – December 21, 1946
And to those Men who made the ultimate sacrifice!
The Chincoteague AVP-24 earned six battle stars during WW II**

The Chincoteague in WWII, covered service at Vanikoro Island, Santa Cruz group. Survived numberous bombing attacks by Japanese aircraft July 14-21, 1943 Vanikoro Island. Served in The Solomon's Campaign, The Marshall's Invasion, Seaplane Tending at Eniwetok, The Treasuries and Green Island. She carried fuel, passengers, supplies, and Air Crews between the Solomons, Gilberts, Marianas, New Hebrides and the Phoenix Islands. Voyages to Guadalcanal, Auckland, New Zealand. Participated in the invasion of Iwo Jima. A long and rewarding service, included duty in Tsing China.

The following personnel killed in aft engine room:
July 16, 1943
1. Lt. Percy A. Weaver E-V (G) USNR
2. Carey W. Berry CMM (PA) USN
3. Carl S. Gobble Jr. MoMM1/c (USN)
4. Chester W. Clofelter MoMM1/C (USN)
5. Harold J. Creeden MoMM (USN)
6. John W. Harp F3/c (V-6) (USNR
7. Jennings P. Herbert MoMM2/c (V-6) (USNR)
8. Carl I. Goodman EM2/c (USN)
9. Hershel E. Stroud F2/c (V-6) (USNR), killed in forward mess compartment, directly above engine room.

Decommissioned: December 21ˢᵗ in Orange, Texas.
Began service's as WAVP-375 (WHEC)-USCGC, March 7, 1949.
Decommissioned June 1972.

I have made an effort to include within the pages of this book, many and varied documents and personal experiences, that relate to this time in history, 1941-1946 in WWII. Some of a very personal nature; others of events related to actual battle descriptions!

CHAPTER 1

(PRELUDE)

As a Seventeen-year-old adolescent kid, aboard the USS Chincoteague in the month of July 1943, during WW II, I would be witness to the violent concreted attacks against our Ship and its Survival, despite being severely damaged by Japanese repeated bombing attacks and the resulting loss of many lives of my Shipmates.

As a result, of those violent times, my concept would be forever changed as to what war was really about. My life would move forward over the next fifty or more years and gradually memories of that event would fade into the recesses of my mind! In the 1980's quite by accident those events would again come into focus, because of a chance meeting of an old friend that propelled me into attending Chincoteague, reunions at various locations.

As we gathered together, relating our experiences from that era, I began to ask questions regarding that period. We were puzzled by the many views of why and what had transpired during the Japanese attacks, why they had suddenly selected our ship. I needed to find answers to the many questions that began troubling my thinking process, so my search began! I started by obtaining Deck Logs and personal crew and Officer Lists for the Chincoteague. This only added more fuel to the fire, as this resulted in the need to go further in my quest for knowledge; more documentation was needed, so back into the National Archives I went.

First would be the Deck and Personal logs from the USS Thornton AVD-11, then the same from the USS Mackinac AVP-12 and that raised even more questions. When the USS Chincoteague had arrived at the port of Espiritu Santos on the 4[Th] of July, 1943, The Captain of the Chincoteague, Ira E. Hobbs reported aboard both the Thornton and then the Mackinac, which was preparing to depart back to the USA, for servicing and maintenance.

On board both ships, Commander Hobbs conferred with the Captains regarding refueling, arming and general information regarding safe anchorages, also general survival techniques that had been employed with their years of service in this war zone. The Thornton, had survived the Pearl Harbor attack on December 7[Th,] 1941 and the Mackinac, was in the same environment for almost two years.

Aboard the Thornton, James W. Beall, SOM2/C was a witness to the conversations between Sellers, Commanding Officer of the Thornton, and Hobbs, Commander of the Chincoteague, regarding the safest anchorages, Enemy activities, and why these actions should be implemented.

Also another person of interest was Lt. Frank D. Langworthy, who was also present aboard the Thornton. I have had conversations with him several years ago, confirming what Beall had reported to me. Another Officer aboard the Mackinac, Lt. (jg) John K. Myhre was also an interested party to conversation between Paul D. Stropp and Ira Hobbs.

Almost the identical cautions and warnings were issued aboard the Thornton. Why Commander Hobbs did choose to set his own agenda, regarding safe and prudent actions that would possibly have had different results for the ship and its crew members. With no prior knowledge or experience as a Ships Commanding Officer, I feel that ones' experience in the conflicts of war would be invaluable to everyone's survival. The decision as to whom or what should be held responsible, for the tragedy at Vanikoro Island, will have to be decided by each person who reads this account. As for myself, my choice has been made!
Bill Armstrong!

CHAPTER 2

(THE FIRST VOYAGE)

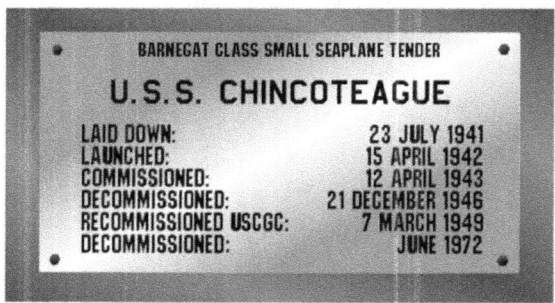

The Vision!

Before the start of hostilities, that engulfed this planet with the start of WW II, in the late 1930's, a group of visionaries, within the military establishment of the United States Navy had seen the need for the development of a special type of vessel, that would have the capability of covering large areas of the Earth's Oceans, and with their mobility, which included small squadrons of long-range aircraft, such as the PBY'S, that possessed the flexibility, due to their capability to land on either the Ocean surface, or could be land based; thus with this ability to move to other locations within a short time period. They felt this would give them a huge advantage to fill the void. As a result, many of the Destroyer type vessels that had been mothballed, after their service in WW1, were in the process of a conversion into vessels of this type to fill this need that existed, prior to the start of hostilities. And so, the AVP- had been created and only too soon would this vision become a reality, after the events of December 7th, 1941 and so, the struggle would begin!

Lake Washington Shipyard
September 3, 1944

Billie R. Armstrong, Farragut Idaho, October 1942

CHAPTER 3

(A JOURNEY TO THE COAST)

As I sat at the window of the train, watching as it slowly moved away from the Naval Station at Farragut Idaho, which had been our home for the last two months; we were just a group of raw recruit from their training session here at this cold watery location on Lake Pend Oreille, in Northern Idaho. It was the latter days of December 1942, and the cold snowy winter was upon us, as we slowly gained speed, I was glad to be inside a warm environment, because you could see the snow being blown along by a cold, blustery wind. Yes! It was winter in Idaho.

We had no idea where we would be heading. Rumors abounded! Seattle, Portland, or other locations further south. I believed that the journey would not be a long one, because sleeping accommodations were not afforded us. This would become a long night. My stomach was really jumpy with the excitement to be leaving the confines of Farragut.

Finally, sleep would overtake my nervous expectations, as to what was awaiting us the next day. A sudden commotion awakened me and I bolted out of my sleepy world, day light had arrived, and as I looked out the window we had arrived inside the Rail yard, but where? I asked the conductor that was approaching, what was the location where we had arrived. Seattle, WA was his reply! A short time the Chief Petty officer, in charge of our group, told us to gather up our belongings and be ready to disembark.

We had finally stopped inside the terminal and then were told to form up in a group, after exiting the train inside the station. So the movement started, as we fell in line and left the train, then moved over to an area some distance away. I was very surprised at the size of this group, possibility thirty or more then; I spotted my little buddy Bobby Hidalgo. I hurried over to his side and was glad to have him there with me. They moved us outside the train station into a cold blustery morning. I was sure glad I had my P-coat on, also my gloves; boy, it was cold in Seattle.

They had several taxicabs lined up for us and we piled in and off we went, destination unknown. After a short drive I could see that our group was headed to the harbor area, and then someone said that our group would be going to Bremerton WA, at the other end of Puget Sound, which was thirty miles south of Seattle.

We were dropped off at the Ferry dock where we would be departing from. The gate was lifted and we walked aboard the Ferry. This was a huge vessel, the name I can't seem to remember. I would find out later, there was a large group of them operating the Sound that was some sixty or seventy miles long. We arrived at our new destination about an hour or so later and then moved into our new home at the receiving station barracks, which would be our new home for the next few weeks or months!

Most of us would become part of the general work force, as being just non-rated seamen; we would be used in many labor capacities; from unloading supplies, cleanup details, and ammunition details. In the hills surrounding Bremerton, were large underground, ammunition storage bunkers where large supplies of ammo were stored in buried concrete bunkers that were not heated inside, with very little lighting. Moving large projectiles from cargo carriers into the cold, miserable unheated damp areas would demand lots of stamina and warm attire (gloves, sweaters, P-coats and wool caps), still it was all you could do to stay warm.

You had to be extremely careful as there was always the danger of Static electricity because those projectiles could create sparks if dropped against each other, which was always present because the outer shell was constructed of steel that contained an explosive substance inside the casing, plus the pointed tip (the firing timer) was constructed of a brass/copper alloy, which made it a good conductor of electricity. They were hard to move in this cold environment; there, temperature would almost be at the freezing point, due to the lack of heat. Fortunately this was not a job that required our help most of the time.

From time to time a few of us would take the great Ferry ride into Seattle, as our curiosity would get the best of our youthful minds, young and adventurous natures, after being kept inside a training camp for those many weeks, this was like going to Disneyland for us, also being young and with our youthful surge, we wanted to meet Girls!

As a result of my curiosity, I found that for some reason, the area to the west of Sand Point Naval Air Station became of interest to me. I had inquired about a location that offered an indoor skating rink, because as a young kid this was something I had enjoyed doing as a pastime with my brother, so the search began. The word was relayed to me that such a location was in the town of Ballard, just over the channel, Northwest of Seattle, not too far from our Sandpoint location

I am not quite sure of the name at this juncture of history in life. I believe it was either the "Ridge Rink, or the Roller Bowl"; anyway, I decided to explore this area one evening and after several bus transfers I finally arrived, then went on inside. After a few minutes I decided to rent a pair of skates and hit the floor. I soon became accustom to the music and the feeling of being back on wheels. Naturally my curiosity had me looking around for young ladies that didn't seem to be under escort, I soon noticed a very attractive young girl, which I began a conversation with.

We seemed to have a mutual attraction and we continued to stay together until she informed me that it was time to go home. I then asked if I could escort her there and she agreed. We boarded the bus and after a trip that consumed about 45 minutes, we arrived at her home in the Ballard district. I thanked her for a very pleasant evening and wished her a goodnight, plus the promise of another date, and then I departed back to San Point. Even after almost 68 years, I can still remember her name, Millicent Mills, her address and phone number!

I enjoyed dating Millicent and meeting her family and Sister Bernice. Her Father worked for the Great Northern Rail Road, as a Supervisor and her Sister worked for the local transportation district. The family was very nice to me and I enjoyed their company. They made my absence from my own family less of a loss. Millicent would be my first "Crush" but as time progressed she seemed to be less and less attracted to me. After the Chincoteague left for other places, despite continuing to send her letters, she never answered them. Slowly over time, her memory left me, but even after such a long passage of time, I don't believe you ever forget that first infatuation.

Later into the month of January, the fury of winter descended on this area with strong snowstorms almost on a daily basis. A crisis was occurring in the area; especially in Seattle, where most of the transportation was almost brought to a halt, due to the huge snow drifts building up within the city itself.

People were unable to travel to their place of work due to this snowy dilemma. The War Management board decided that they needed help from the many military personnel stationed in the area; plus many had heavy equipment that could be helpful; after all we were indeed involved in the war. Many jobs that involved manufacturing products, for this purpose, were being threatened, due to this condition caused by Mother Nature. In the final push as many as fifteen thousand military personnel were recruited to free the city from this wintry grip. Tons of packed snow and ice had been removed from the streets, and other areas, so once again the work could continue.

There also was a problem in the port around Bremerton, due to this same problem. The ice buildup on the loading piers prevented the large cranes from moving on the rails; somewhat like the train rails used, as the cranes used the rail system. So we sailors were recruited to solve this problem with pick, and shovels, working in the freezing temperatures in the late evening and into the early morning hours.

Another sweet little job that we were recruited for was called (De-magnification). I will attempt to clarify. Any vessel that is placed into Dry-Dock, is a system that encloses the ship into its confines. The water is then pumped out, leaving the vessel free to perform any repairs, or hull cleaning, (removing sea growth) from outer hull, that if left to continue growing, would impede the ships movement through the ocean.

During this process in the Dry-Dock, some of the work that was being performed, whether it be repairing, welding, or just regular maintenance, those activities created a magnetic attraction that if not removed would have an influence on the ships compasses and navigation equipment; so after this work or maintenance had been completed and the ship removed from the Dry-Dock back into the harbor, then the process of removing this magnification would begin.

The ship would be placed dock-side, where a work force would proceed wrapping a huge heavy cable around the ship from bow to stern, which after complication an electrical charge would be sent the length of this cable, during a programmed time period to remove the magnification. Handling this very heavy cable became a labor intense process, combined with the freezing weather along with being wet really made for a long and tiring night. It may have not seemed such a task during the daylight hours, but I never had the opportunity to experience that during that time frame. It seemed most of the seamen were doomed to the night shift; seamen, you see, were the Navies labor pool.

A view of the Bremerton Shipyards, sometime in the 1940's

Volume 4   MAY 18, 1945   Number

BUILDING SHIPS TO BLAST THE JAP

CHAPTER 4

(ON THE MOVE AGAIN TO KIRKLAND, WA)

One day in early February, we were informed that we would be moving to another location to the city of Kirkland, WA and should have all our gear packed and ready after breakfast the next morning. The purpose of this move would be to have our new ships crews near the location where it was nearing the final months of its construction. This was the first word that we had heard of what our group had been sent to this area for. Many questions needed to be answered, as to what type of ship that we all had been selected for. We would have all our questions answered tonight, as a special information meeting was planned.

That night, after our dinner, we were told to meet in the Recreation room; there all the facts regarding our new assignment would be spelled out. As the meeting began, a chart was placed on a large screen lighted on the wall. A map was highlighted and the location of our next destination was pointed out. A large portrait of a vessel was placed over the map, then the fellow began outlining information regarding the ship; describing the physical description, layout and detailed information regarding what its duties would cover. After he finished his talk, he asked if there were any questions regarding just what the crew's tasks might be and where we could expect to be deployed when construction was finished.

We had quite a question and answer discussion that lasted for an hour or more. The meeting was closed, and then everyone departed the room to whatever tasks or other areas they wished to visit. Bobby Hidalgo and I joined a small group and went to the Canteen, just to sit around and shoot the bull; also to unwind from all the pent-up excitement from today happenings!

Up at dawn! A fast breakfast, then we went down to an assembly area with our belongings. Our excitement was apparent, as everyone I took notice of was chatting and seemed to be on a nervous high. In just a few short minutes we noticed a large Bus approaching and as it came to a stop we were told to board with our gear, then after a short period of time we departed Bremerton. Would this be our last visit here? I suppose many had that same question in the back of their mind.

We headed to the dock area and soon drove aboard the large Ferry Boat that would take us back up Puget Sound to the Seattle area where the rest of our trip would conclude after we finally reached Kirkland; our new destination and home. As we moved along, after departing the Ferry from Bremerton, about 45 minutes later we approached a large body of water, then someone shouted! Lake Washington! We approached a suspended road structure supported by a large pontoon system. As we began our crossing, I said to myself, what a magnificent sight, a feat of engineering, this young boy was visualizing, so many new different sights in such a short period of time after becoming a part of the Military service. Life had moved so fast, so many things new and interesting, life was so full of exciting new places to view!

Our Bus finally finished its journey over the lake and a short time later entered the small town of Kirkland, not entering the main portion. Just on the outer edge, we entered the small parking lot of the YMCA and were told that would be our new home for a few weeks or so. We disembarked and after everyone had collected his gear, we were led inside the structure. They had erected a number of Upper-lower Bunk Beds that was structured inside the auditorium area was the largest available space that afforded sleeping areas, because this YMCA was not a very large building.

Preparing the Warriors

After life had begun to follow a boring routine, following our occupation of the YMCA,

A few of us would be taken to a location outside the building where a simulated 5'38 Gun Breach had been set up, no barrel, only the projectile loading mechanism was present. A diagram and a small table had been set up, and groups of 3-4 were selected. Then a session of what each part of this mechanisms functions were; the Pointer, the up-down operation, Trainer, side-side movement, Projectile Man, place the live shell into the loading breach (The device that forces the projectile into the breach) Powder Man (Places the powder charge behind the projectile, to provide the explosive force to send the projectile up the barrel.

And last, but not the least, the Hot Shell Man, (after the explosive charge is fired, the hot medal casing is expelled out and away from the breach, this object is very hot due to the explosive ammunition that was incased within this container produces a great amount of heat, so a large pair of asbestos gloves are provided to catch this hot casing, then discard it without being burned).

A sailor was chosen for each of those positions and each day for possibly an hour or more they would rehearse the process; to form a team that would eventually become a well-polished Gun Crew aboard the ship.

After this routine had been established and the amount of excitement to be had in the town of Kirkland was limited, most of the guys started looking to other areas for some entertainment.

I suppose the answer had to be Seattle, just across the lake. The problem was transportation. It was only reachable by a long drive around the lake, or over the floating bridge of the same lake. The other method was with a Small ferry boat that departed at times on a schedule that didn't always favor the liberty hours, so most of our group was not able to use it, but this was about to change.

Over the waters! Sandpoint Naval Air Station!

We were informed that our time in Kirkland was about to end. We would be moving just across the lake to the Naval Air Station of Sandpoint, WA. This was not a stranger to us, because we had attended some classes at this location on several occasions with transportation in a Motor whale boat, which was there for our use, plus other military that moved across on a regular basis. A farewell party had been set up in a location (small building, a dancehall) on the lakeshore, the weekend prior to our departing. It was quite a sendoff, much in the way of liquid refreshment and dancing, quite a party. I am sure many suffered from liquid fatigue the next day!

The main Gate at Sandpoint Naval Air Station, Seattle, WA

Our new home was quite a change, nice accommodations and comfortable bunks, along with great food. Another improvement was transportation. Just outside the main gate, across the street, was the bus stop and this was a joy! The only down side would be the security watches that one had to stand, four hours, but only in the nighttime hours, 8:00 PM-12:00 AM,12:00 AM-4:00AM,4:00 AM,8:00 AM, at the coldest time of the night!

All of your cold weather equipment; sweaters, scarves, wool cap and gloves, finally your Pea coat, along with a rifle, instruction pack around your already crowded neck, all this while trying to slowly march about, and around that area, in a military stance, usually an Aircraft hangar, or other important installation. This only happened maybe twice a month. Thanks for small miracles!

In the latter weeks of March, some warmth began to invade the area. Bobby Hidalgo and occasionally Jay Marchand, from our boot camp days, would venture into the City of Seattle, which had a wonderful transportation system. We had no special destination in mind, just visiting different areas of the city, the harbor area and years later, how this city and San Francisco, CA, so resembled each other in many ways, especially the hilly areas, along with the seaport and the docking areas.

As the year progressed into the first weeks of April, 1943, work had almost finished on our new assignment; The USS Chincoteague AVP-24, was the title that was given to our new infant, soon to be given birth in just a few days. I was full of nervous suspense because I had not yet had a glimpse of the new child and was looking forward to viewing this new addition to the family.

A few days later we had a crew muster on the airstrip at Sandpoint, all in dress blue uniforms and this was, I believe, a bringing together of the complete ship's crew for the first time. Before, we had been scattered at various locations around the area. Now the complete Crew, Officers, Enlisted vets, and last but not least the Boot Camp contingent (Rookies). We now became a Family of One!

The Control tower at Sandpoint Naval Air Station

Aerial view of Sandpoint Naval Air Station, early 1940's

The Christening of the USS Chincoteague (AVP-24) April 15th 1943

Chincoteague farewell dinner Kirkland, WA April 1943

<u>*USS Chincoteague Specifications*</u>

Displacement 1,766 Tons

Length 310'91/2

Beam 41'

Draft 12'5

Speed 17 Kts.

Complement

USN-215

USCG-10 Officers, 3 Warrant Officers, 136 Enlisted

Electronics

Radar: SPS-23, SPS-29D

Sonar: SQS-1

Armament

USN- Four 5"/38 dual purpose gun mounts 1-2 guns on the bow, were closed mounts, the 3-4 on the stern were open

mounts. Four dual 20mm gun mounts located in the upper superstructure, (bridge area).
Propulsion Fairbanks-Morse, direct reversing diesels, two shafts, generating 6,400hp.

The primary duties of the Chincoteague was the refueling and servicing PBY Catalina patrol Seaplanes; replenishing their ammunition, bomb's used against Japanese Bases, Ships and other installations. We also offered accommodations for Aircrew men and Pilots (sleeping, bathing, and meals and flight rations). We, in essence, were a floating Gas station, Ammunition ship, Hotel, Diner and Laundry mat combination.

April 15, 1943. The day had arrived and we were blessed with a gorgeous one with not a cloud in the sky. Many dignitaries gave speeches and finally the Christening. The baby had arrived, fit and ready to be taken into the family of AVP'S. Over the next few weeks they would put the ship through a series of what was called (Shakedown) voyages to discover any birth defects that needed to be addressed and repaired before being declared fit for duty. A few were found.

The journey begins, May 13 1943

We had been moved to Bremerton WA Shipyard, so that the proper attention could be given to any problems found; no outstanding problems had been noted, just adjustments needed here and there and finally we left out of Puget, Sound into the Straits of San Juan De-Fuca, and into the Ocean swells of the North Pacific, turning south. Destination unknown!

Commander Ira E. Hobbs

Commander Ira E. Hobbs was a native of Oklahoma. He graduated from Annapolis in 1925. He had four years of Battleship duty and three years on Destroyers. He has been in naval aviation for 10 years and has served in the North Atlantic, South Pacific and in the Aleutian Islands. He was on the Carrier, U.S.S. Ranger when war was declared. At one time he was Assistant Operations Officer for the Commander of the U.S. Navy carrier forces in the Atlantic area.

Into the open sea (our first voyage to San Francisco after Commissioning) May 1943

We would be in San Diego for the next few weeks, continuing with issues that had to be addressed regarding the ships readiness to move forward into the Battleground, South Pacific. A few minor problems were solved, plus the addition of other Crewmembers, more supplies, etc. I would have time to visit my Mother, brother, sister and the rest of my extended family, before departing once again into the unknown consequences that the war held for us! After a short shakedown cruise, we set sail from San Diego on Sunday, the 13th of June for a destination that was a mystery to all, except our skipper.

We arrived in the Hawaiian Islands at Oahu on Sunday the 20th of June and after we had received a large contingent of Sailors and Marines aboard, we departed on the afternoon of June 22; we headed out again, destination and address unknown!

Looking for King Neptune!

After crossing the equator, we Pollywogs went through our initiation to become Shell Backs (Full fledge Sailors) and then we reached Wallace Island's on the afternoon of June 30, 1944

We discharged a large number of Sailors, approximately 50 or so. We headed out again on July 1st, with the remaining group cf Marines still aboard.

The Chincoteague, AVP 24 arrived July the 4th. 1943 in Espiritu Santos and shortly after arriving at our anchorage, the remainder of our passengers, the Marine unit, was dispatched to their destination.

The making of a Shell Back!

More ceremonially games for the equator crossing

Commander Hobbs on the bridge with crewmember readying himself for crossing ceremonies! June 1943

This plaque, on a rocky outcropping as you enter Espiritu Santos Anchorage

CHAPTER 5

HOBBS, WAR!
(THE TRAGEDY AT VANAKORO*!)*

Our skipper, Commander Ira E. Hobbs reported aboard the Mackinac, AVP 13 to confer with that ships Commanding officer, Commander Paul D. Sropp. This meeting was observed by Lt. (Jg) John K. Myhre, in the bridge area of the Mackinac. During this period, Commander Hobbs conferred with the skipper of the Thornton, AVD 11. Lt. Frank D Langworthy and James W Beall SOM2/C witnessed this conference in the bridge area.

During that period of time, when Commander Hobbs was aboard the Thornton, James Beall would be a witness to the conversation between their Skipper, Commander Sellers and Commander Hobbs of the Chincoteague. During this conversation, Sellers was explaining his choices for an anchorage at the Island of Vanikoro.

He believed the choice Hobbs was about to make was a mistake as to where his anchorage would be, or the prudent one, due to those experiences he had encountered as Captain of the Thornton. He stated that the restrictive space that he would encounter in the smaller confines of Saboe Bay would, in his opinion, not serve him well in a crisis situation and would place his ship and crew in an unpleasant situation during an attack by Japanese forces, either by air or sea.

During their tour of duty in those waters they encountered the presence of Japanese Submarines, with sonar soundings, when they left the harbor. They would send a PBY aloft to scout the surrounding area adjacent to their position and would be at flank speed while leaving the confines of the larger anchorage.

On numerous occasions submarines had been sighted from aircraft going and returning to the anchorage. With no surveillance outside the anchorage of Saboe Bay, their situation would become tenuous at best. During the evening hours nothing would be in place to intercept or prevent a submerged Submarine from entering the harbor and inflicting a mortal blow to any ship that was anchored within the smaller confines, because there was not enough room to maneuver the ship, at that darkened time.

Even if they became mobile, an exit from that area would be almost impossible to navigate out through that narrow channel during those darkened hours making it almost impossible at best! Returning back to those days, more than sixty three years ago when, as a Seventeen year old raw recruit that placed his fortunes within the hands of older and wiser men, it is very difficult to rationalize in my mind the decisions that were made that would have such disastrous results on so many lives, including my own.

The documentation that has been collected and included within the pages of this book were somewhat of a shocking nature, and changed my prospective of those persons that I had trusted to make the right choices while performing their duties. What impact those decisions would have on the families of those that did not return from the war! I must admit that this discovery has had a deep and sorrowful impact on me, but there is no way we can change history, only the way in which we view those persons that were involved in it!

Commander Hobbs had received just about the same cautions from Commander Sellers of the Mackinac and he made his own choice! We departed the following morning at approximately 11 AM for Vanikoro Island in a relief capacity, replacing the Mackinac, as a servicing vessel for the PBY Patrol Squadron stationed there.

It should be remembered that the Mackinac, in conjunction with the Thornton, had decided to use the larger anchorage at Peou Bay for their aircraft servicing duties, because there was a larger area for maneuvering the ship in case of attack by Japanese forces. It also offered a larger extended range for radar surveillance and the ability to execute a hasty retreat from danger. The picture in this book, should give one a view of a much more expansive anchorage that was afforded in the larger, more open area, rather than the smaller, more confining anchorage of Saboe Bay!

The Commanding Officer of the Mackinac tried to explain how vulnerable they would become at that location and why they believed the larger expansive area offered a more secure choice, due to the ship being in closer proximity to the higher mountainous shoreline and would restrict the use of their radar unit from signals in that area. They could only receive signals from that area, directly toward the open expanses of ocean to the southeast.   The Thornton and Mackinac would be exchanging Air-Craft Tending on a rotational basis on average every three to five weeks and had decided to use the larger outer harbor for its plane servicing duties.

And for what reasons we will probably never know, as the more secluded anchorage of Saboe Bay was smaller in area, and could only be reached by traversing a narrow opening inside the reef and also was closer to the Island's shore with less room for navigation. Commander Hobbs chose the more sheltered anchorage. I try, in some way, to understand what motivated his decision to completely ignore those warnings and suggestions put forth by others that had established a safer routine, over the last couple of years that had proven to work, keeping secret their operations from the Japanese!

Were his actions designed to provoke the enemy into a combative environment? As for me, nothing else describes his actions. Did he, in fact, wish to carry his version of war to the enemy? If so, why? What did he believe he could accomplish in such a confined location, using a logical sense of mind. For others aboard the ship that he was committing to his, I believe, less than a rational decision, regarding their lives and safety. Yes, we had all swore to defend our country with our lives, but not waste them in a foolish and careless action that indeed had horrible consequences!

I do believe that Commander Hobbs, had established his own agenda, as to how he would pursue his view of war. With this combination of incidents, that would entice the Japanese into a contest of action, might satisfy his quest for victory. There seems to be no other rational answer for his actions that neglect caution and common sense from advice offered from the former Ships Commanders as a proper course to pursue.

Later in my search into records regarding Hobbs Naval career, I was shocked to discover that he had been awarded the Silver Star for his actions during our battle at Vanikoro, in 1943. I was stunned by this discovery. I feel that a more complete investigation into his action and the outcome may have had different results; possibly a reduction in Rank, but he had orchestrated his own rewards, sadly at the expense and tragedy of others!

The Mackinac, for some time had been at Espiritu Santos, forming up with a convoy to return to the United States on the west coast for overhaul. The ship departed from Espuritu Santos on the 9th of July 1943, and arrived there on the 25th of that month.

At the officers Club on Vanikoro, Island, Ensign Coffey to the right
July 1943

Crewmembers aboard the Chincoteague, Vanikoro Island, Saboe Bay July 1943

Chincoteague Sailors' on the Beach, at Vanikoro Island July, 1943

Armed native soldiers on Vanikoro Island, 1943

The Crew of the Thornton, on Vanikoro, Island Sometime in late 1942 or early1943

U.S.S. Thornton, at Vanikoro Island, Santo Cruz Group

The Governor of Vanikoro Island and natives come aboard
Chincoteague,
As a welcome committee July 6, 1943

***R&R** on Vanikoro, 1942-43 the **USS Thornton** Crew members*

Supplies delivered, aboard PBY, USS Thornton, 1942-43

Servicing PBY at Vaniko 1942-43

USS Sonoma (ATO-12)

CHAPTER 6

(JULY 6, 1943)

We arrived on July 6, 1943. The work proceeded without incident, Until the afternoon of July 14th, that day at about 12:30 pm a plane, Believed to be on a photographic mission, was sighted at an altitude of approximately fifteen thousand feet.

Fire was opened up almost immediately, but the results were undetermined. The ship had left its' anchorage in the harbor and proceeded to the safety of the open sea and remained there for about one hour before returning to the anchorage, after losing contact with the plane.

A comment! Regarding the sighting and Antiaircraft action against this surveillance aircraft. Prior to the arrival of the Chincoteague at Vanikoro, this had been a daily routine by the Japanese air forces, in fact, James Beall, a crew member aboard the Thornton described to me that almost every day this event would occur and you could almost set your watch by this event. He would observe the pilot with a powerful telescope from the bridge area. No defensive action was taken against this observation by any of the Seaplane tenders that preceded the Chincoteague; this had become a routine by the Japanese forces

James Beall informed me, that prior to our arrival to relieve the Mackinac; they along with the Thorton had been very successful with their fueling and arming with not one bombing attack by the Japanese forces. The aircraft would arrive very early each morning, be fuelled and equipped with their Bombs, and be on their way to the target areas almost at sunrise, returning in the late afternoon, refueled then depart back to Espiritu, Santos. So secretive had they been that, until our arrival the Japanese had not a clue as to the location of the home base, from which the attacking aircraft had come!

I think it quiet remarkable that they had kept such a camouflage about their activities over such a long period of time, which to me says that they completely fooled the Japanese into believing they were just a group of sailors, fishing and relaxing at this location!

Prior to our arrival, I'm sure that the actions taken by the Commander of the Chincoteague on this day, was a surprise to the enemy forces, as to the location of the ships anchorage that instigated this behavior, was also a surprise. This was a departure from the normal. I am sure they suspected that this change from the daily events probably was a signal that other actions soon would be taken, so they reacted in an aggressive manor.

This would be the second action taken by Commander Hobbs that was out of character from other groups that preceded the Chincoteague. The first was the selection of a more confined anchorage; secondly, taking defensive action (firing on the Japanese observation aircraft). Third the instruction to the Communications Officer to setup a Radio Beacon for the retuning patrols squadron, which was a total blunder.

Could it be that Commander Hobbs, at the age of forty-three, a former Bomber Pilot, was past the age of flying combat missions and was frustrated by this? So he decided his Ship was not going to continue the lazy, non-combative life style of his predecessors, lying around enjoying the comforts of swimming, fishing and the life of leisure. No! He had made this journey into the South Pacific, to fight the Japanese, the Enemy, no matter the consequences, sounds logical to me, unless he was completely out of touch with reality.

The actions that Commander Hobbs undertook, completely destroyed a very well organized, and functioning operation that had kept Japanese forces deceived, as to the real actions that had been performed under this cloak of secrecy, for the past two years. It had now been destroyed by Hobbs reckless actions, this bastion of deceit formulated so carefully over that time frame, was now useless, never to continue as a forward Observation and attack Base. Just a few months after this incident, it had to be abandoned.

Normal routine was continued through the rest of the day, until 06:47 pm in the evening when a Japanese twin-engine bomber was picked up on radar. The plane, believed to be a Sally type, after circling about for some few minutes, dropped two brilliant white flares about two thousand yards off port quarter from an altitude of approximately fifteen hundred feet.

These flares landed near the entrance of Saboe Bay. During this time no gunfire was used in order to take full advantage of the darkness and to keep our position hidden. Contact was lost shortly after the flares were dropped and life aboard the ship returned to normal. On the morning after the flairs were dropped, the planes returned, with a vengeance.

They released their bomb loads from an altitude of about eight thousand feet. The bombs fell about fifteen hundred yards from the ship, bursting in the jungle to the east of Saboe Bay entrance. Only this one run was made, the planes continued on out of contact.

A few hours later at 11:10, another formation was picked up on radar. This group made a dummy run on the ship and these were thought to be a Sally type and this time there were nine of them flying a close V formation. On this run they passed on the starboard side, heading out to sea.

After circling about, they came in from the sea, passing this time on the portside. The ship got underway immediately by slipping the starboard anchor and at the same time opening fire, but no bombs were dropped, and the planes disappeared eastward.

Five minutes later, at 11:36 they came again and this time it was the bombing run. followed our planes all the way in. It was discovered years after those events, that a radio beacon had been ordered established for the returning aircraft from their bombing mission against Nauru Island by the Communications Officer, so as to assist this bombing group in their return from this target.

This was really something that was a surprise to me, why would you leave yourself so vulnerable to attack by the enemy, as I would find out later, this was not a procedure used by any of the other support vessels that preceded us at this location.

Even if the mission had been successful and had rendered it impossible for aircraft from that targeted area to respond, the slower speed of the PBY'S probably under two hundred miles per hour, would allow the Japanese at other locations to They dropped groups of three bombs each in a pattern, which with our maneuvering placed two groups on our port quarter and one directly astern. No direct hits were sustained, the closest bomb falling about fifty yards from the stern, resulting in some minor splinter damage above the fantail and to the trainers sight of number four 5"/38 gun. The ship continued on out to sea and when contact was lost, it returned at 13:00, in order to receive VP-71 which was about to land for rest and refueling, prior to a bombing mission.

During this and all subsequent actions the guns were by local control, (each gun was controlled and directed by their own crews) as the ship had no directory control system. Control, that was not dependable at this time during the early stages of the war and was not of any great value; also, during the night there had been no activity by the Japanese, but even so there would be no restful sleep during that period of time.

Early the next morning the planes of VP-71 began arriving from their overnight bombing mission. Radar had picked up their IFF identification signals as they came in. The last plane had landed at 07:25am, when the first cluster of bombs from five twin-engine bombers bracketed the ship across the forecastle.

They came from the Northwest, at about eight thousand feet, apparently having react to throw off the aim of the aircraft that were in pursuit.

At 08:05m, a new attack was developing; four planes, coming in from the Starboard quarter. On this attack all the bombs fell clear, because after we were able to reach the open sea, evasive action could be taken by using flanks speed and full Rudder action. When contact was lost, it was necessary to return in order to service and Dispatch those aircraft from VP-71 Santos.

We returned to port at 08:53am, having received orders to return to Santos, we dispatched all of the patrol squadron except those that were in need of fueling. At 10:20 we weighed anchor and stood off the entrance, leaving browser boats to fuel the remaining planes. This event with a beacon to guide them, along with their superior speed they were able to close the gap and follow this Radio highway back to its source!

The ship got underway at 07:26 am, heading out of the bay when immediately thereafter the planes came in from the Southeast on their second run. A cluster of bombs fell about fifty yards astern of the ship then the planes circled off, preparing to make their third bombing run.

At 07:38am, just as the ship was emerging from the mouth of the bay, the bombs struck. The nearest burst about fifty feet from the ship on the starboard side at frame 105; gasoline lines were ruptured and ignited as if they were pyrotechnics in
No 1 M.W.B. (numerous splinter holes were made in the ships side).

 Fire parties rushed to the scene. The gasoline system was blocked off between the rupture and the system below decks and the fires were extinguished by the use of fog nozzles. Fires also started in the living compartments C-201, C-203 and were brought under control by the sprinkler system.

During this time, the ship was moving at flank speed and was not able to make any evasive maneuvers, due to the narrow confines of the channel between the coral reefs. Then at 07:57am the ship was clear of the reef and again was able to take evasive action; before this time, the only recourse would be the changing of speeds

It was our intention to return to Saboe Bay at 15:00 to pick up the bowser boats and personnel. By 11:20 the ship had cleared the reefs and was maneuvering outside the harbor entrance. Twenty-five minutes later another attack came. Five Sally's overhead released their bombs, which bracketed the ship.

A few minutes later after circling about into the sun, they came in again and it was at this point that we received a direct hit from what we believed to be a 100 K.G.delayed action bomb, which had pierced three decks, the super, main, and second before exploding in the Aft. Engine Room!

Forward Mess hall after bomb explosion in Engine Room Below!

During the lull between attacks, we had secured from General Quarters orders to go to condition 2, (an alert with fewer personnel at their battle stations). I had returned to the Galley/ Bakeshop area to help prepare meals and refreshments for those crewmembers still on station at their assigned areas. During this period, there had been no alert as to further air attacks from the Japanese bomber forces.

While I was working in the bakery area and standing in front of the dumb waiter (this devise was used to move food and bake goods to the mess hall one deck below), the explosion occurred in the engine room. The explosive force was so great that it ruptured the decking below the dumb waiter shaft, sending this force up the interior of the shaft, blowing open the door which, I was standing in front of, striking me in the forehead and rendering me unconscious.

I was in this state for approximately 15 minutes and as a result, was left with a huge black and blue lump in the middle of my forehead, about half the size of a baseball and with one hell of a headache. I must add a comment that I had received from one of my shipmates from that era.

Dick Whittington recalls that shortly after the bomb had exploded in the aft. Engine room, he came into the Galley/Bakeshop area and noticed a body on the deck covered with flour and unconscious. He believed it was one of the cooks he was friendly with, but after he had made that statement about the flour covered body, everything flashed back to me, because I was that person on the deck covered with the flour.

I had gone below to the mess hall to retrieve some items there and return them to the bakeshop. Among the items was a container of flour, which I loaded into the dumbwaiter and sent the contents back up to the galley/bake shop, I had been in the process of removing those items from the dumbwaiter and had just closed the door when the bomb exploded and had the container full of flour in my hands at the moment of impact. When the ship had been relieved from general quarters, I returned to the bakeshop to help prepare sandwiches, along with other snacks for those people that were still at their battle stations.

A short time after the bombing, when I had regained my senses, I was curious as to what had taken place after the bomb had struck the ship, so decided, with some sense of fear, to explore that area below deck (a journey that I was to regret for the remainder of my life).

I exited the galley area on the port side of the ship where the bomb had struck and observed an opening in the deck, but was not able to see anything below, due to the lack of proper lighting. I continued along the deck area until I reached the ladder down to the crew eating area and was astounded at what was visible in the mess hall area.

The explosion from the bomb in the area directly below had forced the mess hall deck into the shape of an inverted bowl, bowed upward, and not offering a safe avenue across the deck, so the only choice I had left was to continue toward the hatch opening at the forward entrance to the mess hall. As I came to that hatch opening, I noticed a large area covered in blood, it was there that the bomb had penetrated the deck on its deadly journey into the engine room.

I didn't notice any sign of an injured person in the immediate area. After passing through the hatch, I made my way to the starboard side of the ship toward that side of the mess hall and as I came closer to that area, I noticed a compartment ahead that had an object lying on the deck, covered with a tarp.

I also noticed that this object had a human form. I was somewhat hesitant to enter that area, but proceeded anyway; after a short pause.

When I came closer to the object, the realization hit home that this was indeed a body and why I continued on as I did will never be clear to me (possible some immature curiosity on my part). I reached down and slowly moved the tarp from one end and was confronted by a pair of feet underneath. I then slowly pulled back the other end of that tarp. I was not prepared for what I was viewing, as the body was headless, a horrible sight.

Nothing in life had prepared me for this and due to the stress from the bombings, lack of sleep etc., I became sick at my stomach, because I had become a fairly close friend to the victim, Herschel E. Stroud during my short time aboard the ship.

This episode of viewing the horrible mutilated body of a person that had befriended me would have a lasting effect on me. At only seventeen years of age, it would dramatically change my attitude for some months to come; no longer a childish attitude about this great adventure I had pictured just a few months ago, but a sobering realization that this was not what I had envisioned when going off to win the war.

Seems that Herschel had stepped through the hatch at the exact moment the bomb arrived there; what a horrible act of fate! Even today I have trouble in my mind accepting some of the events that happened during that fateful day, prior to the deadly destruction in the aft engine room.

We had secured from General Quarters (Battle stations) and went to condition #2, which requires just a token force to be at their respective stations, but still be in an alert state of readiness (that means that all departments shall still be at a state of awareness) even with reduced personnel, which includes Gun crews, Sonar, and Radar Operators.

I guess my question is why there was no detection of enemy aircraft in the area just prior to the deadly tragedy in the engine room? I am sure, from all the people I have contacted, that all equipment was in an operational status, so where was the Radar warning? Did some one step away from their station during this critical period? I don't suppose anyone will ever really know the answer to this question, but I personally believe a more aware effort could have prevented this tragedy.

Number four gun went out of commission at the same time, due to water damage and the ship was now moving at a slower rate of speed because of the loss of the aft engine room power and was using only the starboard propeller shaft for the ships power. Furthermore, power was also lost to the steering gear and hand steering had to be used during subsequent actions. At 14:20 another attack developed.

Three bombers came on a run at eight thousand feet. On their first approach they streamed out a series of green flares, while heading into the sun. After circling around they started their bombing run again. The ship opened fire with all guns, and then the ship was bracketed with a series of bombs. At least one five hundred pound bomb fell along the port side, which stopped the forward engine room.

The splinters and concussion produced by this group of bombs resulted in considerable damage to personnel, the ship and boats, one of which caught fire. The remaining guns that were in working order had to be manually operated. Number three five-inch gun reported a Japanese plane had dropped out of formation trailing smoke. This was the only observed damage recorded from our defensive actions. A PBY patrol bomber in the vicinity later verified this.

The ship lay dead in the water, until a final attack occurred at 14:50. A single plane, whose bombs fell two hundred yards abeam made it; so this marked the end of attacks; although at the time, more were expected.

With the aft engine flooded and some aft compartments partly flooded with water coming through numerous openings in the hull, the ship developed a heavy list to starboard; all available men, including the gun crews, were thrown into this effort to save the ship.

Nothing could be done with the aft engine room, but bucket brigades were formed in the flooded compartments at the stern and amidships. Handy Billy pumps were also pressed into action and at 15:00, working without letup, in order to keep the ship afloat. That night the struggle seemed to a hopeless struggle! No power could be restored to allow us to use submersible pumps, but despite all efforts the water continued to rise. It was discovered that in the forward engine room the water level could be controlled at a depth of a few feet; an effort was undertaken to place the engines in working order. The first to respond were the generators. Both the one hundred K.W. and two hundred K.W. started. At 23:00 the main engines were turned over. After one unsuccessful attempt the next one came to life and the ship once again was underway at 23:50.   After sailing about an hour, we were picked up by the Thornton.

THORNTON (AVD 11)

USS Thornton, AVD-11 saved the day

That vessel sent a boat over with additional handy Billy pumps, which were immediately pressed into service. With the Thornton as escort, we sailed for close to two more hours. On two occasions during this period, electrical fires had started and were brought under control and extinguished with CO_2.

Officer on Stern area between bombing attacks

July 1943, on the Alert!

Commander Ira E. Hobbs on Deck, with group of Officers July, 1943

CHAPTER 7

A PERILOUS VOYAGE
(As told by, Henry Franklin Benson Jr.)

In early July 1943 the Chincoteague was given a relief assignment. We were to proceed north approximately 500 miles to the Island of Vanikoro in a relief assignment to replace the USS Mackinac, another seaplane tender scheduled to return back to the United States, for repairs, and reassignment.

We would anchor among the coral reefs near the Island, set our buoys and make preparations to service six PBY patrol aircraft that would arrive from Espiritu Santos each morning. We would refuel them, which would increase their range by approximately 1000 miles further to the north, allowing them to cover a larger area in their patrol assignment during the scouting period.

On the morning of July 16, 1943, we anchored at Vanikoro Island and placed the six buoys in place. The next morning, the six aircraft arrived; we then proceeded to refuel all the aircraft. They then became airborne, continuing on to their patrol sectors, they returned later in afternoon from their patrols. Our small boats refueled all the aircraft and they returned to their home base.

A Japanese Recon Photo Aircraft at a very high altitude had followed them back from their patrol and there was no action taken as the Japanese aircraft left the area.

The next morning, the six aircraft landed and each one taxied to their assigned buoy secured and were waiting to be refueled. Before we could commence refueling the planes, six Japanese Bombers started their bombing runs against the Chincoteague, as it lay at anchor.

The order was given to let go the anchor (chain and all) and a dash to the open sea was started to clear the coral reefs in an effort to get to the wider expanse of the ocean and a more maneuverable position, where evasive action became our ally. The first bombs were just near misses; several fires started, due to explosions very near the ship, but were quickly extinguished. The Japanese made a number of attacks again, at least half a dozen and some damage had occurred, but nothing serious as yet!

We advised Espiritu Santos of our situation being under attack and asked for some fighter aircraft protection from Guadalcanal, but were informed that at this time none could be sent. They told us that they couldn't spare us any fighters, as they had their hands full, but wished us good luck!

The only small boat left on the ship was a 26-foot motor whaleboat. On the 18th, Captain (Ira) Hobbs told me he was going to maneuver the Chincoteague as close as possible to the entrance to Saboe Bay at Vanikoro Island, where I would take our only remaining boat, along with people of my own choosing, (I wanted one of those to be a Chief Signalman). We lowered the boat into the water, with instructions to return to the bay, where we had been anchored and roundup up all the boat crews.

There was 600 gallons of gasoline in a bowser tank in the motor launch. We were to divide up the gasoline to refuel the remaining aircraft, so they could become airborne as soon as possible and head back to Espiritu Santos. Captain Hobbs informed me that he would return the next morning at daylight where they would retrieve us.

I rounded up the boat crews, and then finished refueling the planes and once again they were airborne, returning to their home base. The next morning Captain Hobbs didn't return as promised. I could hear explosions just over the horizon, so I figured he was either sunk or damaged, and wasn't able to return to our anchorage.

I had made a decision that if the ship hadn't returned by the next day, I was going to leave this location with the crew of 15 kid boat crew and my Chief Signalman, then head south. All day we loaded the largest boat (a 40 foot motor launch) with two 50-gallon drums of diesel as extra fuel, and some water.

We left Saboe bay, Vanikoro Island the next morning before sunrise. The Chincoteague still had not returned. I was beginning to question the decision I was about to make leaving the Island, after all the majority of the boat crew were just young kids, but they seemed to have a blind faith in the decision; was I making a huge mistake? You cannot escape the thought that you could be making the wrong choice; anyway, I had selected the option I believed was the right one, so the voyage began!

In the following two days, and night that followed, using the skills that I had developed over the years in my duties as a Quartermaster, that experience, especially during the nighttime hours, guided by the stars, we were able to arrive back near the northern tip of Espiritu Santos, where we encountered the Ocean Tug, in its quest to locate the Chincoteague. Chief Quartermaster Benson, the Chief Signalman, along with the rest of the Boat crew were taken aboard the USS Sonoma, our gear also came aboard. The motor –whaleboat was secured with a towline and so began the trip returning to the Chincoteague.

Their last message received from the Chincoteague was that she was filling with water and had lost all power, and the Destroyer Thornton was alongside removing those crewmembers that were seriously injured. The Sonoma finally found the Chincoteague. Chief Benson and the rest of the crew re- boarded the ship.

Right after we had all returned aboard the ship, we came under attack by the last group of Japanese Aircraft. As they started their last attack—Holy Smoke! Here comes three Marine fighter aircraft from Guadalcanal and after three passes, they shot down all four Japanese aircraft. They informed the Destroyer Thornton, over the intercom that they were at the extreme end of their fuel range and had to make a quick return to their base a Guadalcanal. They dipped there wings, off into the late afternoon sunset, I have been one of their boosters ever sense.

Chief Quartermaster was given a citation for his actions, returning, supervising and refueling of those aircraft at Vanikoro. It states that his conduct "was an inspiration to his crew and in keeping with the highest traditions of the United States Naval Services." It was signed, W.F. Halsey, Admiral, US Navy. "He had done his job and came through alive once again".

Some may question his actions. Surely there was a huge risk factor, many things could have worked against him and I am sure that the probability of Japanese submarines in that area was a real possibility. No one has any doubt as to what would have been the outcome there; never the less, this was a very brave and heroic act!

CQM Benson, back aboard Chincoteague, after rescue by USS Sonoma

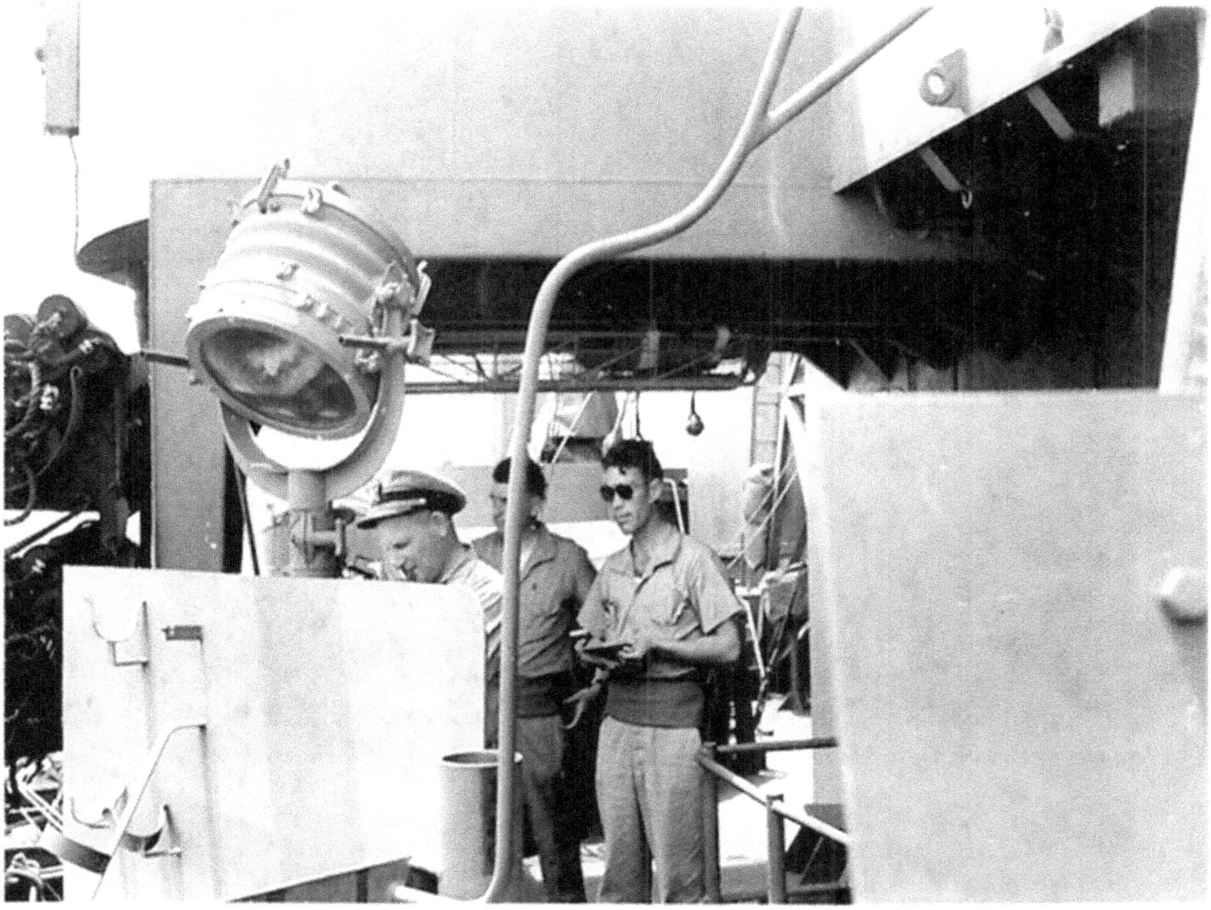

Commander Hobbs, on deck with other Officers

Another Officer looks like he needs a shave!

Hoisting the rescued Motor whale boat back aboard from Vanikoro towed by USS Sonoma

PBY-Aircraft alongside the Chincoteague, to remove wounded crew members and transport them to Espiritu Santos for treatment

The aftermath of battle, shell casings

Between bombing attacks, I am setting on the right behind group, with my Bakers cap on my head

At 02:45, fire started again in the forward engine room, the inboard engine scavenging belt was seen to be filling with oil as well as diesel, it was immediately decided to shut down the engine; however, with excess amounts of oil present on the belt there was no way to secure the engine so it continued to run. With no way to control the speed of the engine, after a few minutes the speed of the engine began to increase and was on course to self-destruction.

It was necessary to remove all personal from the engine room, while the room was in the process of being secured, in an effort to smother the fire and at the same time foam generators were set up.

The Thornton again came alongside, hoses were connected to the fire mains, and foam poured into the engine room.

The fire was fought with fog nozzles and foam until about 05:45 in the morning of the 18th when the last of the foam was used up and the fire appeared to be localized, but was still smoldering. The forward engine room was still battened down and all intakes covered by blankets and mattresses, all hands moved topside, with the exception of the bucket brigades, which continued to function in other areas.

At this time all non-essential personnel were transferred aboard the Thornton, which pulled away in order to take us in tow, at 07:40 the towline was cast off, due to what they believed to be submarine contact. The Thornton moved off and proceeded to drop two depth charges, returning, when contact was lost. Towing resumed at 09:39 and continued until 12:17. At this time the towline was cast off, the ship listing badly to starboard; again the bucket brigades began the tasks, but the flooding could not be stopped.

U.S.S. Chincoteague, Dead in the water from bomb explosion in engine room, July 1943

The stern was now settling low with less than two feet of free board remaining, as the degree of list was varying between twelve and eighteen degrees. Orders were given to lighten the ship, so torpedoes, heavy equipment, machinery, winches, and other heavy gear were jettisoned over the starboard side.

A slight improvement in our list slowly began to show the results from this effort and with the help of additional pumps, flown in by P.B.Y aircraft, along with renewed effort by the bucket brigade, enabled us to check the flooding and eventually right the ship.

During this effort at 13:04, the Thornton again came along the starboard side to furnish power for the submersible pumps, also to receive our confidential and other valuable gear. She remained alongside until morning, refusing to cast off.

CHAPTER 8

Angels with Gull Wings, 17.30-PM

"VMF-241 the Black Sheep"

On the afternoon of July 17, 1943, the squadron was informed that they were to provide air coverage for the battle stricken seaplane tender USS Chincoteague, damaged and dead in the water, alongside the USS Thornton. Bill Pace called a meeting to discuss the plans for the following day.

Pete Folger and Henry Miller worked late that night with their maps, along with the plotting boards to plan strategy for the next day, including the employment of a path finder PV-1 Ventura. With only 2 or 3 hours of sleep, they grabbed a quick shave by moonlight, and started again before 3'oclock the next morning.

Millers division was scheduled for departure at 04:15, but a heavy overcast had developed in the early morning hours, delaying their departure until after seven that morning. Miller and Ledge Hazelwood took off alone following along with the Ventura on instruments, until they emerged out of the overcast.

Their uneventful mission had begun a long day in which twenty-one other pilots, all of them veterans on their first patrol mission, except Tony Eislie, who maintained a series of over lapping patrols over the stricken vessel and if not for a quirk of nature, the day may have ended just as uneventful, at least for VMF-214, if not also for the Chincoteague!

The final flight to depart Buttons late Sunday afternoon was pace's, with Jack Petit, Dick Sigel, and McCall rounding out the flight. They arrived over the Chincoteague at 17:30, which was still dead in the water alongside the Thornton. They commenced to orbit at nine thousand feet, as the daylight began to slowly fade into the late afternoon light.

Seen from above them, the darkness seemed to rise up to them, so that in a few minutes the two ships on the surface below them were slowly being enveloped by the darkness that was fast approaching with the fading daylight, and all the while the four Corsairs were still bathed in the golden light of sunset.

Likewise, any aircraft at an even higher elevation would have even more sunlight, and looking up from the lower elevation, the Marine pilots from their vantage point would find themselves at an advantage and anything above them would be easy to see, enabling Jack Petit to call out a tallyho on three aircraft approaching from the north at twelve thousand feet. Pace, believing they were Ventura's, decided to lead his flight op for a visual confirmation.

To the intruders, actually Mitsubishi GCM Nell's, it must have appeared that four Corsairs suddenly have risen from the darkness below, the twin engine Nell's dumped their bombs early, much to the delight of the crews of the Chincoteague, and the Thornton, and the surprised Japanese gunners opened fire at the marines from an extreme range-more than a thousand yards.

Ignoring those Japanese gunners machine gun fire, Pace continued to climb while Dick, Segal, and McCall split away and maneuvered to catch the bombers between them. The Nell's turned to the right and dived, but they were no matches for the Corsairs speed, as they plunged into the rising darkness.

The Nell on the outside of the turn fell behind, and from fifteen thousand feet, Pace selected it as his target for an overhead run. It was like ducks in a pond. He came down with a full deflection shot, with just the very tip of its tail in the outside ring of his gun sight, and triggered his guns. The incendiaries found the Nell's fuel tanks and the bomber exploded in a huge ball of fire, a spectacular sight in the fading daylight.

Jack Petit rolled in next, selecting the leader of what had once been the V of three planes, but the target proved to be hardier. Petit raked it with a steady stream and was rewarded with a trail of smoke.

He reversed his course, and came back for a firing pass from the front quarter, and reversed again for a fast turn to the left. With each successive pass he achieved more hits, though not to the extent he had hammered it the first time, and much to his frustration, the badly wounded Nell reached the safety of the clouds.

At the same time, Sigel and McCall ganged up on the last Japanese bomber, which was losing altitude fast and was barely visible as it dived into the gloom, Sigel poured solid hits into the Nell and drew smoke, but when McCall's turn came he found that he had a problem. It was April 7 all over again! His Irish luck deserted him again in the form of his guns this time; only one was working.

The whole division had tested their guns after taking off, testing each gun individually, and his had been working. Now only one gun was operating and his pass on the Japanese plane was ineffective. He was thinking the guy in the top turret has more firepower than I have!

The other fighters came around to finish off the last Nell. Dick Sigel came in for a beam run, observing no hits but noticing that his enemy's guns remained silent. No doubt he had hit his target hard on his first run, and perhaps aided by McCall's lone gun.

Finally Bill Pace made a low side run, using the last moments of twilight. He could see that the Nell was smoking, and although he was unable to confirm any hits in the darkening light.

By now it was pitch black, and none of the Marines had any night flying experience or training, making any further pursuit hazardous. Pace turned on his landing lights for a visual aid and ordered his fellow pilots to form up into a formation.

The newly baptized Corsair pilots formed without incident and headed for home, leaving hundreds of jubilant witnesses on two vulnerable warships below.

When they returned to Turtle Bay, Pace and his three grinning Lieutenants gave a full account of their efforts to Pete Folger in the ready tent. The exploded aircraft was witnessed by the whole group that composed the attacking forces, simplifying the confirmation of Pace's claim.

The other two Japanese bombers were smoking, when last seen heading into cloud cover, so Petit and Sigel were given credit for a probable, and after the debriefing, they walked to the evening movie to share their tale, and satisfied that they had blunted the Japanese attack.

Ten minutes later while viewing the movie, it was halted to inform them of a radio message from the Thornton that all three of the aircraft had been seen plunging into the ocean. It would take about two weeks for an official confirmation, but Sigal and Petit had their victories and an even better ending to their story.

The brief, deadly clash over the Chincoteague and the Thornton was a fitting conclusion to the squadron's transition into Corsair's. Major Louis B. Robertshaw; Operations officer for the air group, informed them that they would be returning back to combat in two days, even though the pilots had averaged less than twenty-five hours in Corsairs.

They were desperately needed to support the New Georgia campaign, now that the ground campaign had taken longer than anticipated and in the interim, Command Air Solomon's had maintained constant bombing attacks and roving air patrols against the Japanese in the area, but strong resistance from the enemy was slowly having its effect against VMF-214's sister squadron which was an example of severe attrition. VMF-213 had, during its combat tour over Banika weeks earlier, had begun with twenty-one pilots, but it now had only eleven active pilots left.

That same evening when an air attack developed at 17:34 just as the Jenkins came in sight, three Japanese bombers started a pass at the Jenkins, but just before reaching us, jettisoned the rest of their bombs as they sought to flee. Four corsair fighter aircraft from Gregory Babington's, V.M.F-241 Black Sheep Squadron was in hot pursuit.

I will remember all my life, what a magnificent sight after an exhausting few days, when at times you began to wonder about your ships chances to survive and to have your spirits lifted this way, we watched those Japanese planes, one by one go down in a fiery trail of smoke in the late afternoon light.

That night the ship lay dead in the water with the Jenkins and Trevor, who had arrived 18:20, acting as anti-submarine screen.

Pumping and bucket brigades continued without stop. At 10:21AM the morning of the 19th, the Thornton was forced to cast off. Heavier seas arising resulted in a pounding together of the two ships, producing leaks in the Thornton fire room.

The flooding was now under control aboard the battered Chincoteague and forward engine room fire had died out. The tug Sonoma came alongside at 11:13 with more pumping equipment.

She also had in tow a Chincoteague motor launch, containing sixteen men. These men, left behind at Vanikoro, had fueled and dispatched the three remaining planes, and then decided to head for Espiritu Santo in the open launch. The tug had picked them up while under way to help us. The Sonoma took us in tow at 12:20, from then until we arrived in port a 08:25 the morning of the 21st, nothing of consequence took place.

CHAPTER 9

"THE PERILS OF WAR"

It was during this bombing action that I was to receive several small shrapnel wounds, due to bomb fragments penetrating the steel side of #1 5 Inch gun turret, where I was a member of that forward gun crew on the bow of the ship when a bomb exploded along the port side (left) of our position a large piece of shrapnel from this bomb penetrated the turret wall, was ricocheting from one side to the other as I stood almost transfixed watching this molten fiery object in its wild journey above my head one side to the other, it became fragmented and reduced to smaller particles on this journey.

It was some time later, when things had slowed down, that I found I had received several pieces of this metal in my body, many small fragments in both ankles, some in my chest area another in my back, and in my left hand that is still visible even today. For several years after this incident, while I was taking a shower a small sliver would work its way to the surface of my skin, almost hair thin in size, which would remind me of those days long ago!

From the Diary of William R. Johnson, S 2/C

Wednesday night July 14, 1943 at 8:15 PM, a general quarter was sounded. Sometime later Jap plane at low altitude dropped flare, probably took pictures. 8: AM did not see plane, but bomb exploded on beach, dangerously close but no damage. We pulled out of the bay only to return several hours later. That night 6 PBY'S left to bomb Jap air base. Next morning, Friday at 8: AM, 3 Jap bombers hit us by surprise. Severe damage was done to ship's hull. A little aft of mid-ship was struck with shrapnel in my leg, had emergency treatment.

Again we pulled out of the harbor amid a rain of bombs, circled around in the open sea and then returned to the bay to pick up motor launches and whale boats.

About 11:00 AM they returned again, we once again rushed out of the harbor leaving boat and 9 men behind.

Japs came at us all day (12 attacks) bomb in engine room, killed 10 men, we lay helpless until 4:00AM Saturday morning when the Destroyer Thornton came to our aid, and we bailed and pumped water for two days. The mess hall was a mess due to bomb damage from explosions below in engine room, so with lack of food we lived on pineapple juice.

Sunday, two more Destroyers' came to combat lurking submarines. That late afternoon 3 Jap bombers came at us, but were shot down by our fighter aircraft, which had arrived just in time.

The Fleet Tug USS Sonoma (ATO-12) arrived to begin towing us into Espiritu Santos, where we arrived on Tuesday, July 20, 1943 we moored alongside the (USS Dixie, ad-14) for minor repairs, then placed in dry dock, to continue with additional repairs.

Slept on the beach for several nights, on Friday July 30 was sent to hospital for treatment for leg wound, on Monday had leg x-rayed, piece of shrapnel embedded about 1 inch in the muscle of my leg, surgery was recommended, but the Surgeon decided to leave wound alone.

Saturday, August 7th over half the crew was placed aboard the Dutch Transport Japara; we departed the New Hebrides at 6:00AM Monday morning August 9, 1943 destination United States, and Francisco, CA.

Personal remembrances' from Herb Bacon SOM 3/c July 1943!

I will try to relate my memory of three incidents that occurred during our troubles of July 1943(As the Irish would say) My "Battle Station" was on the Sonar gear, which was located in the CIC room on the Bridge, two of us were assigned there.

When the GQ Buzzer sounded whoever arrived first took the first 30 minutes or so the other was on standby. While in this relief mode I was compelled by a combination of curiosity, and ignorance to step outside on the starboard side of the bridge to see what was going on. (Mostly ignorance I would conclude now).

And there was a 20-MM Gun mounts just outside the Hatch, a friend of mine, Bill Johnson was the trunion operator and phone man on that gun. I was nearby when he took piece of shrapnel in his leg during one of the bombing runs, and relieved he so could seek medical aid in the sickbay for his injury.

On the next bombing run the gunner and loader were also injured with bomb fragments, so became the gunner etc. The planes were out of range for the 20-MM so was never fired, but it always remained a memorable day, much more so for Bill and the other two guys that took the shrapnel.

The next incident occurred shortly after we took that direct hit in the engine room, I know you also have memories of that incident also. My bunk was on the starboard bulkhead just aft of the mess hall, I learned that area was flooded and decide to go down below deck to see if any of my belongings were salvageable, none were. I guess my curiosity got the best of me so decided to wade up to the mess hall and check it out. The first thing I saw was a badly damage body floating in the water. I quickly exited that area in a hurry back towards the bridge.

We were dead in the water, flooded and on fire below deck with no much more than a foot of freeboard on the fantail. Bill Arant, and I were partnered on the boat deck with wrenches' trying to remove anything that could be removed and toss it over the side to lighten the ship. (We were part of a larger group doing this.)

I still remember an exchange between Commander Hobbs, and the Commanding Officer aboard the Thornton prior to the last attacks. Commander Hobbs advised the Thornton's Skipper that it might be wise to take in his lines and move away from us, because we could explode at any minute. The Thornton's Skipper responded to Hobbs "If you have the guts to stay aboard, then we will stay alongside"

Bill and I lived just around the corner from each other in Los Angeles, CA, and ran around together prior to joining the Navy; it was a real coincidence for us to end up on the Chincoteague together.

At some point we looked up to observe Japanese Bombers approaching in the distance, I don't remember either of us speaking----We watched them as they approached, suddenly they made a hard right turn and begin dropping there bombs in the ocean. I looked off to the right and saw the "Corsairs" approaching. I've never been able to properly articulate what took place then. As Rocky said" some up there likes us". Herb Bacon!

Remembrances' from Vanikoro, July 1943
Sherm E. Walgren CRM.

63

The Chincoteague arrived at Espiritu Santos in the New Hebrides Islands, the 4, of July 1943. Commander Ira E. Hobbs reported aboard the USS Tangier, AVP-8 that controlled all activities of the AVP'S in that area of the south pacific.

On the night of July 14 we were enjoying a movie on the fantail of the ship" The moon and sixpence" with Herbert Marshall, about half way into the movie General Quarters, was sounded with bells clanging, on the topside deck (main deck) the total area was illuminated with the greenish light from a flare a Japanese aircraft that was taking pictures.

The ship responded with a few rounds from their 5 inch 38's but with no results. We had none of the newer proximity shells to fire at the time (these were designed to sense objects as they approached with a radio frequency beam. This triggered the explosive charge inside the projectile (we never finished that movie, but many years after the war, I watched it on TV.

Now this is what I observed with my own eyes, (this information is not within the official records) a couple of the bombs exploded just aft of the ship, (maybe at 100 yards). Shrapnel struck several items in the depth charge racks; another struck the optical gun sight on number 4- 5"38 open mount (this gun was not protected with a fully enclosed turret, but was surrounded with a half inch steel shell approximately four feet high). No injuries occurred as a result of this bomb blast, but an individual viewing this sight suffered no injuries. It was a small miracle.

During an earlier attack the fuel pumps on the stern were set afire. Kenny Lubbner became curious about the fire on that portion of the ship and as a result, caught fire and became a human torch. They say he ran and jumped over the lifeline into the sea (this had happened during anchorage in Saboe Bay), and was rescued by crewmembers from a PBY in the harbor.

Charlie Dog, Ransdell, John Shepherd, and I visited him in the hospital in Santo. He was covered in bandages. From what I was told, he passed away a week later.

After the crippling damage inflicted upon the ship, by the bomb blast in the after engine room and with the USS Thornton alongside, decisions were made, that involved the assistance from the Captain of the Thornton, to try and determine the extent of the damage below deck in other areas.

The Captain of the Thornton and me obtained a submersible pump, along with a battle lamp (portable hand held light) and proceeded below deck, into the bowels of the ship together, below the Officers' quarters, and into the bilge that was waste high with sea water from the ships flooding.

As I was moving about slowly in this area, I felt something brush my leg. I focused the light down on this object and against my leg were the remains of a human head that had been severed from the body of Hershel Stroud as the bomb had descended on its path of death into the aft engine room.

When the bomb came thru the main deck, it sliced the length of a watertight hatch, between two mess halls, and exploded against the phone booth in the aft engine room. On its fateful journey to that location, it had decapitated Stroud and left the remains of his head here in this watery tomb.

I dropped the pump into the water, and the skipper of the Thornton made a rather hasty retreat up the ladder (stairway) to the main deck. My costly watch had been ruined, during the trip into the murky foul waters of the bilge; I would expect that many watches had suffered the same fate, during those hectic days.

During this time of mass confusion and terror, while we struggled to survive the possible loss of the ship, our Commanding officer was back on the stern (fantail) on a hunting expedition, shooting Sharks. I suppose, to him, it seemed the proper thing to do, but it seemed rather a foolish pastime, as many of this crew may well have to abandon this ship and it didn't seem proper to add chum (blood) to the water they may be swimming in.

Orders were given to lighten ship. Everything that was movable was shoved over the side. We had six aerial torpedoes, and the three on the starboard side were sent to the bottom At 13:30(1:30PM) a PBY aircraft landed alongside with more submersible pumps, and then began transferring confidential and other gear, over to the Thornton.

At 17:30(5:30PM) flooding was under control. At 17:40(5:40PM), after just a few minutes had passed, three Japanese bombers were sighted, with four F4U's (Corsair Fighters) in hot pursuit. We observed bombs being jettisoned by the fleeing Japanese aircraft.

As the bombers disappeared in a westerly direction into the gathering late afternoon clouds, one by one were seen to spiral down slowly from the cloud cover trailing a plume of fire and smoke. All crewmembers that witnessed this spectacle (some seven to ten miles away in the fading light), let out a mighty cheer, as if watching their favorite team score the final winning run in the ball game.

At 18:30(6:30PM) the ship had righted its self and was once again on an even keel (level) The Jenkins circled the Chincoteague (anti-submarine patrol), then at 19:00 the USS Travers arrived to increase our safety margin for the reminder of the day and to secure the rest of the night.

The next day the Eighteenth, of July at 09:00(9:00AM) the USS Sonoma came into view. She was to take us in tow and return us to the safety of Espiritu Santo for safety and repairs. She was returning from Guadalcanal and while coming to our rescue had spotted the remaining Chincoteague crew members, who had been left at Vanikoro to finish re-fueling the remaining PBY aircraft left there.

With the help of a few of the natives there, we were able to remove the fuel tanks from the boat. They believed that the Chincoteague had been sunk by the Japanese attack, so they were trying to find their way back to Espiritu Santo. The Sonoma spotted them and returned to the Chincoteague, with the boat in tow.

The Sonoma took us in tow and at five knots the return voyage was un-eventful. When we finally arrived we were placed in dry dock, where the remaining water drained from the ship. Recovery teams were sent into the damaged engine room to retrieve our shipmate's bodies; which were then placed in sea bags.

After this emotional task I was able to descend into that decimated area of the ship, it was unreal. The bomb had exploded in the telephone booth, but the phone was still on the hook. The engines had been moved completely from their mountings, and the control had been blown to bits, but the remaining sections of the panel had been left intact, along with the instruments remaining there. A three-inch Stanchion (post) was bent, but a 16-gage (thick) sheet metal vent wasn't even affected. It was strange!

On July 22nd, this message was sent to Comfairwing, 1. Holding services, for deceased Chincoteague ships personnel tomorrow morning at 09:30(9:30AM) if convenient to you would appreciate your visit before 09:00(9:00AM) or after 12:00(12:00PM), as I would like to attend the services.

Submitted by Sherm E. Walgren

Due to the severe damage that we had received during the Japanese air attacks, and repairs that had to be made, while the ship was in dry-dock.

There was no way to do the repairs that needed to be done to make the ship sea worthy .We had no means of propulsion due to the bomb damage in the after engine room, also the forward engine room was in such a state that the only recourse was to make the ship as sea worthy as possible while in dry dock at Espiritu-Santo.

The decision was made to repair as much of the damage hull as was possible while it was here, then to hoist aboard a source for electric energy (a portable diesel generator) for lights and power to operate the ships defenses, radar, fire control and other needs, Etc. Then we were to be taken in tow by an ocean going tug.

It is worth noting that after the Chincoteague's harrowing experience at Vanikoro Island, a decision had been on the table, for some time, regarding the movement from Vanikoro to a more forward area as the war had escalated to other areas closer to those activities and due to the loss of stealth and secrecies, by the actions of the Chincoteague, it made that area a maintenance and service base, to a forward area, some 250 miles to the northwest a reality. Supplies and equipment were being relocated to this forward area in the Solomon Islands, known as Ugi Island; this was to be the final mission from Vanikoro.

"The long road back"

A skeleton crew was placed aboard the Chincoteague, and the remaining crewmembers were sent aboard a cargo ship, the SS Japara, a Dutch freighter bound for the U.S. We departed Espiritu-Santo Monday morning, the 9th of August 1943, arriving in San Francisco on September 11, 1943. After arriving back in the United States, the ship was taken into Mare Island Ship Yard and placed in dry-dock for extensive repairs that would take the better part of 6 months. Just before repairs were completed, around 15th of October 1944, I was transferred to Treasure Island Receiving Station for reassignment.

Photo # NH 97709 USS Chincoteague on 15 December 1943, port side forward

OFFICIAL PHOTOGRAPH

NAVY YARD MARE ISLAND. CALIF

Bow View of USS Chincoteague in Dry dock Mare Island Ship Yard during repairs from Bomb Damage December 1943

Awards and Medal Presentation, Mare Island Shipyard USS Chincoteague 1943

Picture illustrates the hundreds of bomb fragment holes, filled with wooden plugs

Photo # 19-N-57482   USS Chincoteague on 27 December 1943, port bow view

The photograph, shown below, captures the Chincoteague on 27, December 1943 at Mare Island, shipyard after extensive repairs, due to bomb damage in the after engine room in July of that year.

During this repair operation a Mare Island, a decision was made to modify the ships defensive armaments, as it had proven ineffective against Japanese air attacks, so changes were made as follows!

Number two forward 5"/38 mount was removed, and replaced by one quad 40 mm gun mount. One of the two remaining 5"/38 on the stern was replaced by single dual quad 40mm mount, and four dual 20mm gun mounts.

A16-3

Serial ( )

UNITED STATES PACIFIC FLEET
AIRCRAFT SOUTH PACIFIC FORCE

C-O-N-F-I-D-E-N-T-I-A-L

THIRD ENDORSEMENT to
CO, USS CHINCOTEAGUE
Conf. ltr. AVP24/A9
ser. 048 of 25 July
1943.

Subject: Narrative of Action and subsequent events from
            14 to 21 July. (cont'd.)

- -

5.   Commander Aircraft, South Pacific Force cannot close
without expressing his admiration for a splendid piece of seamanship
and a superb fight against heavy odds in which all hands examplified
the best traditions of the Naval Service.

                                        AUBREY W. FITCH

Copy to:
   ComFairSouth.
   ComFairWing One.
   CO, USS CHINCOTEAGUE.

Individual Awards

Purple Heart (KIA and wounded 16 July 1943) – Combat Action Ribbon (retroactive to crew members attached on 16 July 1943)

Name Armstrong, Billie R

(Name in Full Surname to the Left)

3831658   Rate S 2/c   USN.

(Service No.)

Date Reported Aboard April 12, 1943.

U.S.S. CHINCOTEAGUE(AVP24).

(Present Ship or Station)

~~HOUGHTON, WASHINGTON~~

(Ship & Station Reported From)

8-10-43:   Served on board with dis-
tinction during repeated bombing
attacks with resultant casualties,
fires, flooding, loss of light and
power, July 16-21, 1943 and for
bringing ship to port for which the
Officers and Crew were commended by
Commander Fleet Air Wing ONE.

I. E. HOBES, Commander, U. S. Navy.

Billie and Mother in San Diego, CA 1943

CHAPTER 10

(WHERE IS IRA E. HOBBS?)

Many of the former crewmembers that were aboard the Chincoteague, during its commissioning date and the action events at Vanikoro that led to the casualties following this disaster, including officers, had been transferred to different locations, schools, new construction and just different naval locations. During the time the Chincoteague was at the repair facility, Mare Island, CA, Commander R.A.Rosasco replaced Commander Ira E. Hobbs as commanding officer. At this time the whereabouts' of Ira E. Hobbs was not a big concern for the crewmembers, because other matters needed to be addressed. The ship had many serious repairs that needed to be resolved; so we moved ahead to finish the tasks.

Lt. Henry F. Benson

This is a letter from one of the Officers that was transferred to the new construction, according to his children some years after the war!

In the fall of 1943, his father had been promoted to Ensign and he was to report to a new Aircraft carrier under construction in the United States. "I was sure that the war would be over by the time the new ship construction was completed, plus all the sea trials, etc., before the carrier finally was ready to take aboard the new air squadrons and go through all sea trials with them. Surely the devil wasn't going *to* get me now. I was dreaming.

While I was on route to my new ship, I was advised by a Naval Dispatch approximately as follows: "BENSON'S ORDER MODIFIED X ACCEPT COMMISSION FULL LIEUTENANT X PROCEED BY COMMERCIAL AIR X SAN DIEGO WEST COAST X REPORT USS KITKUN BAY AS SHIP'S NAVIGATOR X CONFERM ON ARRIVAL X

The Kitkun Bay was a new smaller aircraft carrier. It was "about 10,000 tons," my father related, carried almost a thousand crewmembers, counting air squadrons. We operated about 50 planes; 25 fighter aircraft and 25 bombers. We usually operated with five other carriers and a screen of six or seven destroyers. All together (six carriers), we could put in the air 200 fighters or 200 torpedo bombers, a sizeable force. "The destroyers and carriers had good anti-aircraft protection (40mm, 20mm and 5-inch guns). Surface fighting was left to battleships and cruisers. They carried the bigger guns."

He didn't know at the time, he stated, "but I was to start a tour of sea duty in the Pacific that was going to involve the Kitkun Bay in the greatest naval battle in history; the battle of Leyte Gulf, the start of the campaign to retake the Philippine Island. In early 1944, the Kitkun Bay saw its first action in campaigns to retake Guam, Tinian and Saipan, which included air attacks by Japanese kamikaze pilots, but my fathers' ship was not damaged.

In early October 1944, the Kitkun Bay was anchored in the harbor at Guam, taking on fuel and supplies in preparation for the next landings in the Philippines. "The narrative continued." While at anchor I received the following message: LIUTENANT BENSON, WILL YOU HAVE LUNCH WITH ME? X SHALL I SEND A SMALL BOAT? X CAPTIAN IRA HOBBS, COMMANDING OFFICER, AND GAMBIER BAY. The Gambier Bay was a sister ship of the

Kitkun Bay. Needless to say, I accepted the invitation. Captain Hobbs was my old skipper aboard the Chincoteague and probably did more than any other person to promote my Navy career, after the battle at Vanikoro. I had a real enjoyable lunch and visit with Captain Hobbs. He had been my Commanding officer, but I always considered him a friend and really admired him.

The landings at Leyte Gulf involved hundreds of thousands of US service personnel and the largest naval armada ever assembled. The Japanese formed a large force of their own to try and blunt this landing and thus; developed the largest naval battle in history, which took place over several days, at various locations over vast areas of land and sea and involving different elements of the US naval air and land forces.

As it turned out, my father's group of ships supporting the landings faced the blunt of a strong and surprised Japanese attack, which caused heavy damage to the American forces; if the Japanese had pressed home their attack, instead of finally breaking off contact and retiring, they could have laid waste to the landing ships and personnel on the beaches

The Kitkun Bay was operating with five other carriers, the USS Fanshaw Bay, USS Gambier Bay, and USS Kalinin Bay, USS St. Lo, USS White Plains and their destroyers USS Hole, USS Johnson, USS Keermann, USS Samuel B. Roberts, USS Raymond, USS Dennis and USS John C. Butler. Their operating positions were guarding the entrance to the San Bernardo Strait, just north of Leyte landings, on the morning of October 25th, my father said.

A large Japanese force, that included four battle ships and five heavy cruisers, had slipped through the San Bernardino Strait and into the Philippine Sea undetected during the night and suddenly bore down on my father's group of escort carriers, destroyers and destroyer escorts. The American carriers, under heavy fire, took flight, while the destroyers and destroyer escorts laid smoke screens and attacked the much larger Japanese forces.

The carriers launched their aircraft, which also attacked the Japanese ships, sinking and damaging some of them. Before it had ended, with the Japanese suddenly breaking off the action and retiring to the north, the Americans had suffered heavy losses, including the loss of the Gamier Bay and its Captain, Ira Hobbs, my father's friend and mentor. During this running battle, the Japanese had fired at the Kitkun Bay but missed. Kamikaze aircraft also later attacked it, but no serious damage was inflicted. Yet again, my father had survived.

That December, while assigned to assist in fueling some other US navy ships, the Kitkun Bay, along with a force of other carriers, battleships, cruisers and destroyers, ran into a severe typhoon. All were low on fuel at the time and riding high in the water, he said. The Kitkun Bay's deck was about 70 feet above the ocean's surface, he noted, but during the storm, huge waves were crashing over the ship's deck.

The Kitkun Bay was designed to survive a maximum roll of 38 degrees before capsizing, my father said. During the storm, he relates that at one point, his ship was rolling to an angle of 36 degrees. The worse winds of the storm at its' peek velocity was measured at 124 knots, or 140 miles per hour. Some ships had capsized, during the storm, with the loss of many crewmembers.

"The Final total"—790 dead or missing, 80 men seriously injured, 146 aircraft were blown overboard or damaged beyond repair." A Navy board of inquiry, studying this weather disaster, recommended that the Navy improve its typhoon warning service and meteorological forecasting. Following this, the Kitkun Bay took part in the US landings in the Lingayen Gulf on the island of Luzon, about 200 miles north of Manila in the Philippines. Kamikaze aircraft again attacked my father's ship, on the way there.
One Kamikaze dived into the Kitkun Bay, just striking the ship at the waterline
Portside, He carried two 500-pound bombs under each wing. One exploded at the waterline, blowing a large hole in the ship, causing flooding and fires. The remainder of the task force had to depart, because they were landing in Lingayen the next morning.

The damage control discovered that the second Kamikaze's 500-pound bomb, was unexploded and lodged in a coffer-dam (a void space between two sections of below-deck compartments). The bomb was between our gasoline fuel tanks and our ammunition storage section. We had to abandon ship, which were about 900 men. Again, about 80 of us in the salvage crew remained aboard. After removing our crew, two destroyers left the area with our survivors.

Back on the ship, we still had an unexploded 500-pound bomb. Another destroyer took us in tow. We had no power, but the flooding was under control. We had requested a bomb-removal squad to come aboard, if necessary, to disarm the bomb and remove it. They came aboard (three fellows--and what a dangerous job awaited them). They examined the bomb and advised us that indeed, this was an armed bomb. (Bombs usually automatically arm themselves, after being dropped from an airplane and this way, they are not as dangerous to handle). When armed and unexploded, the bomb is dangerous to handle. Sometimes just a jolt will cause the bomb to explode.

During the night, we sewed several bodies into canvas sacks. The Captain held a brief service and the bodies were committed to the sea. "Our crew was brought back two days later and we were towed out to sea. There was still a lot of fighting left to be done, but for the Kitkun Bay, the war was over." So my father had survived the war. For his service, he received a number of individual and unit citations.

Starting out at the bottom, as an enlisted man in the Navy in 1931, he rose rapidly in rank during the war, when high casualties helped accelerate promotions. He ended his naval career around the end of the World War II, as a lieutenant in the Naval Reserve. My father always spoke fondly of his naval service, which clearly was among the highlights of his life. I was glad that he had done his job during the war and served honorably. For that, his children and grandchildren can be proud of him.

USS Kitkun Bay (CVE) 71- 1945

USS Kitkun Bay being attacked by Japanese Kamikaze aircraft 1945

A special note regarding Captain Ira E Hobbs, He was not a casualty during the sinking of the USS Gambier Bay. He would become the Executive officer (second in command) aboard the Makin Island (CVE-93). In October 1945 and would become its' Commanding officer.

USS Makin Island (CVE-93) 1944

Photo # NH 94877   Celebrating 1000th landing on USS Makin Island

Commander Hobbs, shown with crewmembers as a group in celebration ceremony at Makin Island 1945

Capt. Ira Hobbs presents Bronze Star to LtJG John Highfill

Captain Hobbs, October 1945

Lt. Kinashi Takakazu.
I-19 Japanese Submarine
Second Commanding Officer July 15, 1942 WW II

Japanese Submarine I-19 WWII

After talking to James Beall about the things that happened during WWII, the subject of those Japanese Submarine raids, along the coast of California, and Oregon in early 1941 came up. During this time period, he was in training at the port facilities in San Diego, CA to become a Sonar operator. This was before he became a crewmember aboard the USS Thornton, AVD-11. He explained that as a regular routine, they would be at sea outside the harbor area, with help from a submarine, using sonar-detecting equipment, aboard a destroyer, as trainees. During one of the episodes, the lookout had noticed a large flotatio.n of lumber, covering a large ocean area surrounding the ship. His response upon sighting this debris was "There's a pigeon setting on that wood." This kid was a southern boy, who had never seen a seagull before. This was finished wooden products, not scrap. So where had this came from?

The answer, a torpedoing of the SS Absaroka, a lumber carrier, just off the coast of California, near Pt. Fermin, San Pedro, CA. There is some contradiction as to the exact location and distance from the coast, when this attack occurred. Some suggest the ship was 26 miles out, but eyewitnesses' describe hearing the explosion and witnessing a huge plume of water spray about 100 feet in the air. This would limit that distance to just a few miles. Although it was severely damaged by this attack, the ship didn't sink, due the large amount of lumber stored inside.

The crew managed to abandon the ship safely; one person was killed by lumber stored above deck capsizing, as the ship began listing, crushing him in the process and falling into the ocean. This was the Japanese Submarine, I-19 pictured above; this would not be the last episode of this nature. On December 25th, 1941 the I-19 was shadowing another vessel, the lumber schooner, SS Barbara Olson, launching one torpedo, that make contact on the seaward side, passing under the ship exploding and on the other side

Submarine Torpedoes Freighter off Point Fermin

American Lumber Freighter *Absaroka*   Jane Russell Posing in the Torpedo Hole   Japanese I-19 Submarine

Actress Jane Russell, standing in damage, area January 26 1942 Torpedoed, by Japanese submarine I-19 December 24, 1941 off Pt. Fermin CA. The card she is holding, state, "A slip of the lip may sink a ship"

Surviving crewmembers from torpedoed vessel SS Absoroka, January 1942

A historical Record of a Japanese Submarine Actions during WW II

Billie R Armstrong!

10 November 1941: Operation "Z":
At Saeki Bay, in the Advance Expeditionary forces, Vice Admiral Shimizu Mitsumi (former CO of ISE), CINC Sixth Fleet (Submarines) convenes a meeting of all his commanders aboard his flagship, the light cruiser KATORI. Ltd.Cdr. Narahara and the other commanders are briefed on the planned attack on Pearl Harbor.

1 December 1941:
The I-23 lags behind the main group after losing one shaft. The AKAGI questions the I-19 about the location of the I-23. 2 December 1941: The coded signal "Niitakayama nobore (Climb Mt. Niitaka) 1208" is received from the Combined Fleet. It signifies that hostilities will commence on 8 December (Japan time). Mt. Niitaka, located in Formosa (now Taiwan) was then, the highest point in the Japanese Empire.

7 December 1941: The Attack on Pearl Harbor:
The I-19 patrols 110 miles NE of Oahu during the air attacks on Pearl Harbor.

After the air attack, the submarines, of the Advance Group, serve as navigation aids for crippled Japanese aircraft returning to their carriers. After 1040, SubDiv 2 is detached from the Kido Butai and subordinated directly to Headquarters, Sixth Fleet. All three submarines are deployed to the area 300 miles E of Maui. **8 December 1941**: The I-19 passes through the area where just the day before, the I-26 sank the 2,140-ton steam schooner CYNTHIA OLSON. I-19 pulls alongside the OLSEN's lifeboats and passes some food to the survivors. Then the I-19 departs the area.

I-19, -9, -15, -17, -21, -23 and the I-25 surface and set off at flank speed after the carrier. **December 11, 1941:** The I-19 is twice spotted by aircraft from the USS ENTERPRISE (CV-6) but manages to crash-dive. **December 14, 1941:** After the unsuccessful pursuit of the carrier, the I-19 and the other submarines, joined by the I-10 and the I-26 are ordered to sail eastwards to the West Coast of the United States and attack American shipping.

The Imperial General Headquarters orders the IJN to shell the U.S. West Coast. Vice Admiral Shimizu issues a detailed order on the targets. I-15, -9, -10, -17, -19, -21, -23, -25 and the I-26 are each to fire 30 shells on the night of 25 December 25, 1941. Rear Admiral Sato, aboard the I-9, is charged to execute the order.

22 December 1941:
Off Point Arguello 55 miles north of Santa Barbara, I-19 chases the 10,763-ton Standard Oil Company tanker H. M. STOREY for about an hour and then fired two torpedoes with 2-second intervals. Just then, a third torpedo starts a "hot run" and it has to be fired as well. All the torpedoes miss. The tanker escapes. 22 December 1941. Admiral Yamamoto Isoroku, CINC, Combined Fleet, postpones the Christmas Eve attack until 27 December.

25 December 1941: The I-19 torpedoes and misses the lumber schooner BARBARA OLSON, steaming toward San Diego. Later that day, off Point Fermin near San Pedro, the I-19 torpedoes, hits and damages the McCormick Steamship Company's 5,695-ton American lumber carrier ABSOROKA, but the ship is towed and beached at Fort MacArthur. The sub chaser USS AMETHYST (PYC-3), on patrol off the Los Angeles Harbor entrance, depth charges the I-19, but without effect. 27 December 1941. Most of the I-boats off the coast have depleted their fuel reserves. Vice Admiral Shimizu cancels the shelling.

26 August 1942: 200 miles SE of Guadalcanal. At 14:25, while running submerged, the sound operator reports contact with several approaching ships, including an aircraft carrier, battleship, cruiser and several destroyers. The Task Force, including the USS WASP (CV-7), is heading north, but once again, Kinashi's approach fails. 29 August 1942. I-19's floatplane reconnoiters Santa Cruz Island, Solomon's; the pilot reports the presence of a destroyer and six flying boats.

31 August 1942:
Starting at 8:15 PM, the I-19 shells Gracious Bay, Ndeni for about 10 minutes. There seems to be a difference between the Japanese dating of events, regarding this engagement. According to their timing, this event occurred the evening of August 31, 1942, but in my research into the deck logs of both the Mackinac and Ballard, this attack was dated the 12th of **September 1942:**

A description of events follows: despite constant evacuations, alerts and numerous search plane losses, the Mackinac setup base at Gracious Harbor in the Santa Cruz Islands in August 1942. Early on the morning of September 12, 1942, two Japanese submarines surfaced at the harbor entrance to shell the Mackinac and Seaplane tender Ballard (AVD)-10 and their seaplanes. The two Seaplane tenders retaliated, but neither side suffered any damages.

September 1942: At 9:50AM, while running submerged, the sound operator reports a contact with many heavy screws at 12-18S, 164-15E. Kinashi orders I-19 to periscope depth. He makes a sweep with his 'scope but no ships are in sight.

250 miles Se, Of Guadalcanal, Captain (later Admiral) Forrest P. Sherman's USS WASP and Captain Charles P. Mason's (later Rear Admiral) HORNET (CV-8), are escorting a reinforcement convoy of six transports, carrying the seventh Marine Regiment from Espiritu Santo to reinforce Guadalcanal. The carriers are steaming in sight of each other about eight miles apart. Each carrier forms the nucleus of a task force. Captain George H. Fort's (later Rear Admiral) battleship USS NORTH CAROLINA (BB-55) is with the HORNET task force to the NE of the WASP force.

At 10:50AM, Kinashi raises his periscope again. This time he sees a carrier, a heavy cruiser and several destroyers (Rear Admiral Leigh Noyes' Task Force 18) bearing 045T at 9 miles. Kinashi estimates the task force's course at 330 and begins a slow approach. The Americans, zigzagging at 16 knots, change course to WNW. Then at 11:20AM, the target group again changes course -this time to SSE. The WASP makes a slow left turn into the wind to launch and recover her aircraft - and heads toward the I-19.

Kinashi estimates that his target is on course 130 degrees making 12 knots. At

11:45AM, from 50 degrees starboard, he fires a spread of six Type 95 oxygen-propelled torpedoes at the enemy carrier from 985 yards. Two or possibly three hit the WASP and start an uncontrollable fire. The HORNET force continues right turns to a 280-degree base course. Suddenly, an alarm is heard from the tactical radio speakers. "The USS LANSDOWNE (DD-486) in the WASP's screen... torpedo headed for formation, course 080!"

At 11:52 AM, a torpedo from the I-19's salvo hits the NORTH CAROLINA in her port bow, abreast of her forward main battery turret. The blast put holes in the side protection, below the armor belt and the NORTH CAROLINA takes on a thousand tons of water. She has a five-degree list, but counter flooding quickly levels her and she makes 25 knots.

At 11:54 AM, a torpedo hits the destroyer O'BRIEN's (DD-415) port quarter and another just misses the HORNET. I-19 dives to 265 feet under the carrier's wake. The first depth charge explodes six minutes after the last torpedo hit. Soon the depth charges were exploding all around. American destroyers try to surround the I-19 to attack together and finish her off. They rain down 30 depth charges.

At noon, the WASP's avgas tanks explode. At 3:15 PM, two cruisers and destroyers abandon the WASP and withdraw to the south. At 3:20 PM, Captain Sherman orders "Abandon Ship". The carrier is scuttled by five torpedoes from the LANSDOWNE and sinks by the bow at about 9:00PM. The WASP suffers 193 killed and 367 wounded.

The USS Wasp (CV-7) fatally wounded from torpedo attack by Japanese submarine I-19 September 15, 1942

Another casualty, torpedos attack by Japanese submarine I-19 September 15, 1942.
The Destroyer, USS O'Brien

2 May 1943:

Off the Fiji Islands, the I-19 torpedoes and damages the 7,181-ton American freighter WILLIAM WILLIAMS. The torpedo puts a hole 40 x 30 feet wide in her port side. The crew abandons ship, but when the submarine does not come back, most of the crew reboards her. They get up steam and make Suva, Fiji with the help of the USS CATALPA.

The Liberty ship William Williams, entered Suva harbor in the Fijis with her after gun deck awash and her bow sticking off the water at a 30 degree angle, as a result of the Japanese torpedo attack. Her crew, performing what officials at Suva termed "a miracle of salvage," had succeeded in repairing water and electric light lines under water in the engine room by Jury rigging a rudder and, by manning the pumps 24 hours a day, they brought the stricken vessel 500 miles into Suva under her own power.

The crew later volunteered to continue salvage operation. They pumped the vessel out and accompanied her over 2,000 miles to Auckland where they continued to aid in the repair work. The damaged merchantman was then able to sail again

18 November 1943:
The I-19 reports the results of the recce flight. **20 November 1943:** American Operation "Galvanic" - The Invasion of the Gilberts: The Americans invade Tarawa and Makin Islands. The invasion fleet of 200 ships includes 13 battleships and 11 carriers.

50 miles W of Makin Island, at 20:49, Cmdr. G. E. Grigg's USS RADFORD (DD-446) makes night radar contact with a surfaced submarine at 8 miles. At 9:30 PM, the RADFORD loses radar contact as the submarine submerges. At 9:40 PM, the RADFORD makes sonar contact and then makes seven depth charge attacks. Postwar, Japanese records confirm that the submarine sunk at 03-10N, 171-55E is the I-19.

Captain Iwagami is promoted Rear Admiral, posthumously. Lt Cmdr. Kobayashi is promoted Cmdr., posthumously. **2 February 1944:** Presumed lost with all 105 hands in the Gilberts area,1 April 1944: Removed from the Navy List.

22-24 June 1986:
Four former crewmembers of the I-19 (Dr. Miyazawa Juichiro, Torpedo men, Tange Shichiro, Otani Tadataka and Quartermaster Sugiyama Rishichi) participate in the USS NORTH CAROLINA reunion in Wilmington, North Carolina. They are presented with a framed fragment of the Type 95 torpedo fired at the NORTH CAROLINA, in September 1942

CHAPTER 11

"BATTLE OF MIDWAY AT FRENCH FRIGATE SHOALS"

James W. Beall, Sonar man First Class Photo taken January 28th 1947
Yokosuka, Japan

By James W. Beall-Sonar man First Class aboard the USS Thornton-AVD-11

James "Jack" W. Beall was born in Tulsa, Oklahoma, 7th of September, 1923. He joined the regular Navy the day after the Pearl Harbor attack. He served 5 years, 10 months and was discharged as a Sonar man First Class. In civilian life he was an Elementary Teacher, Counselor, and Administrator. He retired from the educational service in 1985 near Muskogee, Oklahoma, and has been very busy traveling, hunting, fishing, building his own house and enjoying his friends and family. Here is Jack's description of his ship's mission and his personal experiences in the Battle of Midway at French Frigate Shoals.

In the movie the "Midway" there was a scene on the bridge of a Japanese Flagship. An officer reported to an Admiral that the scout seaplanes could not land and refuel from their submarine, located at French Frigate Shoals. An enemy vessel had taken up station at the Shoals, denying them their refueling sight. That vessel was the USS Thornton AVD-11. The Thornton had deployed to this location, because the Navy had broken the Japanese code and knew they were coming.

The Thornton had left Pearl Harbor around the 28 of May, 1942 and arrived at French Frigate Shoals on the 29 of May. Le Perouse Pinnacle is a large very white volcanic rock that dominates the area and from a distance looks more like an old frigate; hence the name, French Frigate Shoals. The Shoals are not much in land area; a good storm can easily wash over them. A small bay, protected by shallow waters with a narrow entrance, looks as if it would provide the ship with a good anchorage. We had no idea what was going to take place at the Shoals, but we had a feeling it was going to be big. You didn't cruse at flank speed in order to get to the party!

At this time the Thornton was still a prewar ship. She had no radar or sonar. Air defense was four water-cooled .50 caliber machine guns mounted on the galley deckhouse and what .30 caliber rifles were on board. For surface fire she had two, 4-inch 50 mounted fore and aft. With no radar the ship relied on a number of sky and surface lookouts-it even had crow's nest watch (in June, after Midway, the ship entered Pearl Harbor Navy Yard for a complete overhaul and outfitting).

As we cautiously entered the narrow passage into the bay, Harold O'Connor, at his special detail station on the forecastle, was calling out the markings on the fathom line. The water was so clear you could not judge the depth. The ship made a good anchorage and the watch was set. Preparations were then made for the boat and I was a part of it.

With the passing of 60 years, some of the details are missing, yet, somehow I have been able to keep a copy of our orders and by reading them it gives a good jog to my memory.

Just before sunset we started our watch in a 26-foot motor whaleboat with a crew of four. We were to patrol on a line 323 degrees Magnatic-143 degrees Magnetic, approximately half way between the ship and La Perouse Pinnacle. If we saw an enemy sub or plane, we were to open fire with our two Browning Automatic Rifles and our 1903 Springfield Rifles. If we saw a submarine or periscope we were to ram it headlong at full speed, even if this meant the sinking of the whaleboat. Additionally, we were to attempt to lasso the periscope with a line and a lighted buoy. We also had aboard a lighted landing "Tee." The "Tee," shaped like a plane, was to be held, into the wind, to aid a plane in distress to land or ditch. One Very's pistol with red and green and white rockets provided emergency signals.

The wind and surf were a bit high at times, in those shark-infested waters, so it wasn't always a smooth ride. In fact, the alternate crew ran aground one night and had to be rescued by another boat. I believe they used the Captain's Gig to pull them off the beach, after one our officers swam into them with a line. I was eighteen years old at that time this was happening. Because I was on watch at night I usually had some free time during the day. One day, I went with the boat crew to the beach to take provisions to the 13 Marines stationed there. They had no shelter to speak of and were just dug in. Their main weapon was a single 37 mm anti-tank gun. I remember them as a laid-back bunch.

They helped me run a large sea turtle down and turned it over on its back to immobilize it. With the help from the boat crew, we drug it back to the whaleboat and took it to the ship. It made some fine soup for the ship's crew!

These waters were full of sharks, big sharks, so the next day I tried to catch one. I took some scraps of turtle meat, put it on a large shark hook, attached it to a short chain and a block of wood to keep it on the surface, and then tied this to a long piece of marline. I threw it off the fantail and it wasn't 5 minutes before I hooked a 12-foot shark. I really didn't know what to do with it, until the ships Dr. wanted to bring it up on deck. Captain Kline had the Chief gunners mate shoot it with a .30 caliber rifle then, with depth charge boom, we brought it aboard. The Dr. cut it open with one of his scalpels. In its' stomach, we found three large albatross, a rolled up towel with a bar of soap in the middle and a number of large ham bones, that the Dr. jokingly told us were human bones. We cut the jaw out for the teeth and I still have one.

We were at French Frigate Shoals about nine days, then left there for Pearl Harbor. When we got back to Pearl, we began to get a picture of what had transpired over the last week. At that time we did not realize that we had been a small part of what was to be called the greatest sea battle in history! Over these many years, I have likened our small to: "For the want of a nail the shoe was lost. For the want of a shoe the horse was lost." The Thornton had taken the Jap's Nail!

Large pinnacle of Coral Reef, strikingly white

I believe back in the 16th and 17th centuries, viewed from a distance, this was mistakenly believed to be a sailing vessel called a "Frigate; "hence the name "French Frigate Shoal's'

Remembrances' from December 7th 1941
Elbert A. Vowell

Elbert A. Vowell joined the navy, July 14, 1941 in Little Rock, AR, and server six weeks in boot camp in San Diego, California, company 90. In early September, he boarded the USS Saratoga for transportation to Pearl Harbor and permanent duty aboard the USS' Thornton, avd-11. The Thornton was a seaplane tender, converted from an old four-stack destroyer, a relic from WW I, but was assigned various other tasks such as; target towing for subs or aircraft, transporting a hundred or more soldiers or marines to an island a few days away, patrolling and escort duties.   We made roundtrips to places such as Palmyra Island, Midway Island, Hilo and halfway to the states, for standby duties.

On December 7^{th,} 1941, we berthed at a pier at sub base in Pearl Harbor. The Japanese attacked various targets in the harbor; Ford Island, the navy yard and nearby Hickam Field, but ignored the Thornton. We sustained neither damage nor injuries. I was a seventeen-year-old deckhand. My battle station was the sky lookout, located above the bridge and charthouse. I was given an excellent view of the attacking Japanese torpedo planes as they came very low, just above the water's surface, dropping their bombs, just off the fantail. I can still see those torpedoes, as they headed for the battleship row. While we were not prepared for battle, our machine gun crews did manage to get into action against some of the torpedo planes, as did other ships in the area.

One of the attacking aircraft exploded nearby. The concussion was unbelievable, but as I looked toward the source, I saw small fragments, also a large section of one wing slide into the water. We all claimed credit for the kill, but I don't think anyone will ever know just which ship or ships actually deserved credit. The Hulbert, our sister ship, was nearby as was the Sumner. The Latter was, I believe, a repair ship, but our veterans were impressed with the amount of firepower she put up that morning.

More memories related from December 7th 1941 "James Coffey"

In a letter to his son "Jeff Coffey", dated December 6th 1997, he wrote! Fifty-six years ago tonight, I was a bright and eager to learn, young cadet officer in the USC&GSS Explorer, moored to the one and only pier at Midway Island. We had just completed an extensive two-month charting of the entire atoll. The ship was scheduled to sail 0n 7th December to conduct similar surveys of Johnson and Wake Islands

When I went on watch as OOD at 0400 7th, December, I was a 19-year-old kid. When I was relieved at 0745 7th December, 1941, I was aware that something out of the ordinary was going on in Hawaii, but the news (via commercial brdc'st freqs.) was garbled. News traveled slowly back then and we sailed at 12:00 for Johnson Island. Sometime, in the early afternoon, we were advised that Pearl Harbor had been attacked and a state of war existed.

The entire crews of the ship were West Coast sailors and no one had an inkling of what had been occurring in the Atlantic for the last two years. I personally prevailed upon the CO to steam without lights after sunset on December 7th. He was most reluctant to do so, because he didn't want to be in violation of any rules of the road. Needless to say, I was a much older man by the time I went to bed that night.

The second bombing of Pearl Harbor, March 4, 1942

While involved in researching information for the publishing of my first book, relating to mine and others' recollections of events, during the war years 1944-45 in the South Pacific, while attached to CASU-F-20 in the Marshall Islands, during WW II. Many of the small Islands that were bypassed, had become bombing targets for both the Navy and Marine air groups, were Wotje, Atoll. Within the many articles that were discovered would be about Operation, a reconnaissance of Pearl Harbor. This was to access the damages and status of repairs after the surprise attack of December 7th, 1941.

To say that I was surprised at what was within those documents, was somewhat of a shock, would be an understatement. During almost twenty-five years of research and probing within the National Archives and other sources, there was never a mention of this event that appeared before my eyes. I do believe that this was another blunder by Military Secret Services and was such an embarrassment that it was kept a secret over the many years, after the event had happened.

One must remember that after the December 7th event, we as a nation had become a country, reeling in the tragic aftermath of this horrendous blow delivered on our nation. So this was quite a shock to find, but now the meat of the article is, as follows!

A Japanese Naval operation in World War II, that was intended as a reconnaissance of Pearl Harbor and a disruption of the repair and salvage operation, following the attack of December 7, 1941, evolved as planned on March 4, 1942, but was an unsuccessful attack, carried out by two Kawanishi H8K "Emily" flying boats. This would go down as the longest distance ever attempted by two-plane bombing mission and the longest ever attempted without fighter plane escort.

The planning for this operation was formulated in the week following the December 7 attack on Pearl Harbor. The Japanese Imperial Navy command felt they should follow up that first attack by using the long-range capabilities of the long-range H8K flying boats. They planned to bomb both California and Texas. This was being discussed, when the need for information, as to the status of repairs, at Pearl Harbor took precedence. An overall decision was made, that was of the most urgent information needed. Repairs to the docks, yards and airfields of Oahu would help the staff to access American project ability for the months to come.

Their first thoughts were to use five of the H8K aircraft in this mission. They would fly to the French Frigate Shoals, the largest atoll in the Northwestern Hawaiian Islands, some 480-560, miles northwest of the main island group, where they would be refueled by a submarine that would be waiting at that location at the appointed time. Then after this process had been completed, they would continue on with the final phase of the planning. If this mission proved to be successful, further raids would be made.

In proposed replay of events, just prior to December 7 attack, American code breakers warned that the Japanese were reading for a reconnaissance and dispirited raid, then refueling at French Frigate Shoals, and again was ignored by those in authority. When the time approached for the raids, only two of the large flying boats were available for use. Pilot, Lieutenant Hisao Hashizume was in command of this mission; Ensign Shosuke piloted the second aircraft. There were sent to Wotje Atoll in the Marshall Islands, there each aircraft was loaded with four 550-lb bombs.

From that location, they flew 1,900 miles (3,100 km) to refuel at the French Frigate Shoals, and then continued on with the mission 560 miles (900 km) distance. In addition to their reconnaissance mission, they were directed to bomb the "Ten-Ten"dock (a name given for its length, 1,010 feet) at the Pearl Harbor Naval Base, to interrupt salvage and repairing work. However a comedy of errors followed on both sides!

A Japanese submarine, I-23 was ordered to support a fueling location itself, just south of Oahu in a "lifeguard" and weather spotter status for the flying boats, but disappeared and was lost after February 14. American radar stationed on Kauai, then at a later date on the Island of 0ahu, began tracking the two aircraft as they neared the main Hawaiian Islands, which initiated a response by Curtis P-40 Fighters.

PBY Catalina Seaplanes were also dispatched to search for the Japanese Aircraft carriers that were suspected of launching two aircraft (not knowing the type of aircraft involved, and assuming that they were smaller attack aircraft! However; heavy overcast and thick cloud cover hindered this search. (This heavy overcast which was below the flight path of the H8K) became a hindrance to the defending fighter aircraft in locating the Japanese aircraft, which were flying at an altitude of 15,000 feet.

The same cloud cover also became a problem for the Japanese aircraft pilots. Using the Ka'ena Point lighthouse for a positioning point fix, Lt. Hashizume decided on attacking from the north. Ens. Sasao didn't receive Lt. Hashizume's orders, so instead changed course to skirt the southern coast of Oahu. Lt. Hashizume had lost sight of the other aircraft and was only able to view very small patches of the Island below. He decided to drop his four bombs on the slopes of the Tantalus Peak, (an extinct volcano cone to the north of Honolulu) between the hours of 2.00 & 2.15AM.

It was impossible to view the facilities at Pearl Harbor on the island of Oahu due to the blackout conditions being conducted. Lt. Hashizume's bombs landed some 1,000 feet from Roosevelt High School, leaving some craters 6-10 feet deep and 20-30 feet across. Damages were minimal; just a few broken windows.

Most historians and other officials also believe Ens.Sasao, to have eventually disposed of his bombs in the ocean, or somewhere off the coast of Waianae near the sea.

Approaching Pearl Harbor, The two flying boats then preceded their long return trip back to the Jaluit Atoll, also a part of the Marshall Island Group. A long and grueling journey!

There were no American casualties that resulted from this Japanese attempt to bomb and slow any repairs to those facilities damaged during the previous attack, on December 7, 1941, but hopefully a wakeup call to all branches of the Military establishment that this was just a sample of what means the Japanese would use, in their effort to subdue this giant, before we fully awakened to Japan's aims to become the dominant power in the Pacific areas of the world, including territories they intended to swallow in their quest.

Japanese attempted to use this raid in a propaganda crusade, following a so-called unsubstantiated Los Angeles radio report of major damage at "Pearl Harbor", with 30 or more sailors killed, along with many civilians, injured. In an effort to hide their incident and not reveal the truth as to the real culprits, the Army and Navy attributed responsibility on each other for jettisoning bombs into Tantalus.

Another armed mission, planned by the Japanese High Command, scheduled for March 6 or 7, was of the many delays to the first mission and damages to Lt.Hashizume's aircraft and the aircrew's exhaustive state.

A further mission Operation was due to begin on May 30, to gain further intelligence on the location of U.S. Carrier forces, prior to Japan's planned Battle of Midway. However, now the Americans had become aware that the French Frigate Shoals had become a real possibility for a Japanese organizing point, and naval patrols had been increased, per Admiral Chester Nimitz's decree.

A Japanese submarine had observed two American warships at anchor there, prompting Japanese plans. This would result in the Japanese inability to observe U.S. Navy activity, or to keep track of the movement of American aircraft carriers. This action to deny the Japanese access to French Frigate Shoals for an observation station would, in the long term, have a resounding effect on the future Battle of Midway.

Kawanishi H8K "Emily" Flying boat

CHAPTER 12

THE THORNTON'S DEMISE, FATE!

From mid-December, 1944 until late February, 1945, the Thornton was station at Pearl Harbor. On Feb 22nd, she was underway, preparing for the assault on Okinawa. She stopped at Eniwetok in early March, then on the move again to Ulithi, the staging area, preparing for the invasion of Okinawa in early March.

On April 5th, while operating in the Ryukyus as part of a search and reconnaissance Group of the Southern Attack Force, The Thornton was involved in a collision between USS Ashtabula (AO-51 and USS Escalante (AO-71. This incident occurred during the darkness of the late evening. Her starboard side was severely damaged, open to the sea. On April 14th, she was towed into Kerama Retta Harbor. On the 29th, a board of inspection and survey recommended that the Thornton be decommissioned, beached and stripped of all useful materials as needed, then abandoned.

She was beached and decommissioned on the 2nd of May, 1945. Her name was struck from the Navy List on August 13^{th,} 1945. In July, 1957, the Thornton's hulk was abandoned and donated to the government of the Ryukyu Islands. There were a number of casualties, including some of them deceased, but the total amount is unknown, as of now!

PICTURE SHOWS THE THORNTON BEING TOWED INTO KERAMA RETTO HARBOR APRIL 14TH, 1945

USS THORNTON IN KERAMA RETTO HARBOR, APRIL 14, 1945. NOTICE THE GASH IN THE HULL, JUST FORWARD OF THE STACK, FROM THE COLLISION.

This picture shows the severity of the damages inflicted on the Thornton, as a result of the collision at sea April 5, 1945.

CHAPTER 13

USS Sonoma (ATO-12)

It's strange how the fortunes of war have a way of determining the fate of those ships, and the people that were involved in its struggles. In July, 1943, while returning to Espiritu Santos from her duties in and around Guadalcanal, they had no prior knowledge, regarding the plight of the USS Chincoteague, which was in a desperate state from the bombing attacks by Japanese aircraft, earlier in that month.

She had received a frantic radio message for assistance, before entering the anchorage at Espiritu Santos. She abruptly reversed her course to answer this need for help. Shortly after beginning this response, they discovered the motor-whaleboat from the Chincoteague that had left her former anchorage at the Island of Vanikoro with a refueling crew aboard.

After, recovering the crew and taking the whale-boat in tow, she proceeded on her journey to assist the Chincoteague and attempted to take the ship back for repairs at Espiritu Santos. Upon arriving at the location of the Chincoteague, the rescued refueling crew again joined the rest of their crew members, back aboard the ship. Now the Sonoma surveyed the damaged ships dilemma and began setting up the necessary equipment to tow the Chincoteague back to the safety of Espiritu Santos, which they accomplished over the next couple of days.

The Sonoma departed for Lae, New Guinea, where she was involved in those actions in that area during the New Guinea operations. During the remainder of 1943, she operated in and around the Buna Harbor at Papua, New Guinea. She then departed for Milne Bay. From there she took in tow the APC-4 to Brisbane, Australia, arriving there on February 1, 1944. Following overhaul and repairs, she was once again under way and on February 15, returned to Milne Bay, New Guinea.

After spending most of March 11, 1944 around Milne Bay, she departed for Manus in the Admiralty Islands. Spending most of the next three months there, the Sonoma was designated ATO-12. Later that month she moved to the Hollandia area, where she continued her towing duties. In September, she was part of the offensive against the Japanese in the Dutch East Indies Operations.

She suffered a broken crankshaft and proceeded to Gila Bay for repairs. On October 1, she sailed back to Humboldt Bay, where she, once again, resumed towing services. On

October the 14, she became part of the Task Force LI, Task Unit 78.2.9, bound ultimately for the Leyte invasion of the Philippines. The Sonoma entered San Pedro Bay, Leyte Gulf, on the 20th of October. On the morning of the 24th, she opened fire on several Japanese aircraft with her starboard guns.

Crashed into by a burning Japanese Bomber

As she was castoff from the merchant freighter, she was moored next to the SS Augustus Thomas, when a flaming Japanese bomber crashed into Sonoma's starboard side amidships. Two explosions followed immediately and she began taking on water, at an alarming rate. LCI-72 and (ATF-83) came alongside the stricken tug, extinguished the fires on her starboard side and removed the casualties. The (ATF-83 Chickasaw had made a heroic effort to reach the Sonoma, but was unsuccessful in this attempt to beach her on Dio Island. That afternoon, the Sonoma sank in 18 feet of water off Dio Island. Her name was struck off the Navy list in November, 1944. It was a sad ending for such a valiant little ship which had in fact, been a contributor to salvation for the USS Chincoteague.

Walter Jagger, 1944
The Japanese prisoner of war

In July of 2004, I attended a reunion of wartime personnel that were on the USS Chincoteague in Vancouver, WA. At one of the meetings, I told the group about my Hawaiian Invasion Dollar, autographed by Cpl. Abe and asked if anyone had any additional information about his transportation aboard the USS Chincoteague (I didn't bring the dollar, but later sent copies to the interested crew members and researchers.) The reunion attendance was small and only one person attending was aboard the ship during that period of transportation.

His recollection differed from mine in some significant aspects, which is not surprising because it had happened such a long time ago. Cpl. Abe was captured off Wake Island by a submarine. This led to questions about the identity of the submarine, to which I had no answer. Fortunately interest by the crew about my verbal story, prompted me to start documenting and verifying my recollection of the event associated with the transportation of Cpl. Abe and culminated in the account document in the proceeding section, Frank Murphy, of Vancouver, WA, who attended the reunion, became interested and said he had a copy of the USS Chincoteague deck log of that era and if I could supply him with a specific time frame, he could supply me with a copy.

UNITED STATES SHIP ___CHINCOTEAGUE___ Tuesday 19 September 1944
(Day) (Date) (Month)

0-4 Anchored outside seadrome area, SAIPAN HARBOR, SAIPAN ISLAND in MARIANAS group in 12 fathoms of water with 45 fathoms of chain on deck to starboard anchor. Anchor bearings: "tall stack" 162½° T., "Bm" F 114½° T., "Bm" G 086½° T., "white target" 142° T., ships head 017° T. Ship in condition readiness III mike able.

E. KOYT,
Lieut., U.S.N.R.

4-8 Anchored as before. 0700 Secured from condition III mike able.

EINER A. MAY,
Ensign, U.S.N.

8-12 Anchored as before. 0800 Mustered crew on stations; no absentees.

K. B. HOFSTRA,
Ensign, U.S.N.R.

12-16 Anchored as before. 1345 Making preparations for getting underway. 1404 Received aboard as Japanese prisoner of war. Abe, TSUCHIMATFU Cpl., age 28, enlisted, date of capture 1 September 1944. For transportation per orders port director, AGF, APO 244. 1406 PCS 1455 came alongside to port to receive fresh water. 1412 Commenced discharging fresh water to PCS 1455. 1418 PCS 1421 came alongside port side PCS 1455 to receive fresh water from this vessel. 1428 Commenced discharging fresh water to PCS 1421. 1508 Completed discharging fresh water. PCS 1421 took 1500 gallons and PCS 1455 took 1500 gallons. 1513 PCS 1421 cast off port side PCS 1455. 1514 PCS 1421 cast off port side. 1515 Underway in accordance with C.T.U. 57.7.2 secret dispatch No. 190311 of September 1944. Operating as task unit 57.15.2 commander, U.S.S. CHINCOTEAGUE, PCS 1455, PCS 1421 in task unit. Escorting SAIPAN ENIWETOK 11 convoy including the following ships: LST 398, OLE ROLVAAG, H. WEIR COOK, WOLLGAM N. BYERS, JOSIAH SNELLING, convoy commodore in LST 398. Captain and navigator on the bridge, Captain has the conn. Steering various courses and at various speeds to clear SAIPAN anchorage area. 1536 Set condition of readiness III mike sugar, materiel condition baker below the second deck.

K. B. HOFSTRA,
Ensign, U.S.N.R.

16-20 Steaming at various courses and speeds as before. 1600 Took station ahead of convoy, changed course left to 090° T., 089° PGC, 086° PSTGC, 093° PSC, steaming at 2/3 speed 10 knots 132 RPM. 1645 Cut out No. 1 and No. 4 main engines, with No. 2 and 3 on the line. 1700 Took departure from SAIPAN with NAFUTAN POINT bearing 000° T., at two (2) miles. 1905 Changed course right to 099° PGC, 100° T., 098° PSTGC, 104° PSC.

JAMES M. MERRILL,
Ensign, U.S.N.R.

20-24 Steaming as before on course 099° PGC, 100° T., 098° PSTGC, 104° PSC, at 2/3 standard speed 10 knots, 132 RPM. 2000 On station bearing 100° T., 1500 yards from guide LST 398. 2236 Radar indication 240° T., 4300 yards, despatched PCS 1421 to investigate.

EINER A. MAY,
Ensign, U.S.N.

UNITED STATES SHIP _____ CHINCOTEAGUE _____   Sunday 1 October _____, 1944
                                                          (Day)   (Date) (Month)

0-4   Steaming singly enroute to PEARL HARBOR on course 083° T., 082° PGC, 064°
      PSTGC, 065° PSC, at full speed 16.5 knots, 231 RPM., on four main engines.
      Underway in accordance with confidential letter No. A-4-328/JHB/JDR/ port
      director Navy 3237 of September 24, 1944. Ship in condition of readiness
      III mike sugar, material condition baker. Operating independently under
      ComAirPac. 0100 Advanced ships clocks half (½) hour to plus 9½ time zone.

                                              K. B. HOFSTRA,
                                              Ensign, U.S.N.R.

4-8   Steaming as before on course 083° T., 082° PGC, 064° PSTGC, 065° PSC, at full
      speed 16.5 knots, 231 RPM. 0639 Sighted numerous friendly aircraft. 0730
      Changed course to 000° PGC, 001° T., 338° PSTGC, 343° PSC.

                                              W. B. WILSON,
                                              Lieut., U.S.N.R.

8-12 Steaming as before on course 001° T., 000° PGC, 338° PSTGC, 343° PSC, at full
      speed, 231 RPM, 16.5 knots. 0843 Radar contact land bearing 013° T., at 54
      miles. 0955 Sighted two aircraft carriers, recognized as USS. SARATOGA, and
      USS. RANGER, their A.A. guns firing on target. 1004 Projectiles from A.A. guns
      landed close aboard. Changed speed to flank, 260 RPM, 18 knots, changed course
      left to 310° PGC, 311° T., to clear firing range. 1013 Changed course right to
      010° PGC, 011° T., 350° PSTGC, 357° PSC. 1016 Changed speed to full 231 RPM,
      16.5 knots. 1053 Sighted OAHU ISLAND bearing 350° T., at 17 miles. 1143
      Changed speed to standard speed, 205 RPM, 15 knots.

                                              JAMES M. MERRILL,
                                              Ensign, U.S.N.R.

12-16 Steaming as before on course 011° T., 000° PGC, 350° PSTGC, 357° PSC, at stand-
      erd speed 15 knots, 205 RPM. 1157 Reduced speed to 2/3 , 132 RPM, 10 knots.
      1214 Lying to waiting for permission to enter harbor. 1243 Entering channel to
      PEARL HARBOR passing bouys 1 and 2 ., steering various courses and speeds to
      conform with channel. 1311 Passing over degaussing range on course 004° PGC.
      1324 Moored port side to Fox 1 Dock, FORD ISLAND Naval Air Station PEARL HARBOR
      T.H. with three quarter inch head and stern wire and four six inch manilas, all
      lines doubled. 1410 Received telephone service from dock. 1540 The following
      Officers and man disembarked having completed transportation in accordance with
      orders from U.S. Naval Air Base Navy 3237 of 16 September 1944: BONNER, Norman L
      2575551 Ensign, USNR, CANTER, Ralph R Jr. 269481 Ensign USNR. CULVER, Robert's S
      258 515 Ensign USNR. KYLE, Gordon B. 269481 Ensign USNR. HOWITT, John E. Ensign
      USNR. NORALL John B. Ensign USNR. SILVER , Richard L. Lieut., (jg) USNR.
      NOVAC, Michael (n) 85189552 Flc USNR.

                                              W. B. WILSON,
                                              Lieut., U.S.N.R.

16-20 Moored as before. 1600 Published the findings and sentence in the case of
      WILLIAMS, Oliver Jr. 556444 USNR tried by deck court for disregarding lawful
      order and behaving in disrespectful manner to superior officer, finding: Guilty;
      sentence, confinement for twenty days on bread and water with full ration every
      third day and to lose $16.00 pay per month for period of three months T.L.P. $48.
      Sentence approved by convening authority. 1640 Transferred Prisoner of war
      Abe . TSUCHIMATE, Cpl., Japanese Army captured 9-1-44 to 14th Naval district
      Marine Forces. Entrusted to E. C. BOSBYSHELL , 1st Lieut., USMC. after completion
      of transportation per orders port director AGF. APO 244.
                                              W. B. WILSON,
                                              Lieut., U.S.N.R.

20-24 Moored as before.

                                              K. B. HOFSTRA,
                                              Ensign, U.S.N.R.

This could confirm the certain dates for Abe's transportation aboard the ship, using my date parameters could provide us with the information to pinpoint the submarine in question. Within two weeks he sent me copies of the appropriate deck log entries, which verified my recollection of the important aspects of CPL. ABE transportation, particularly the sequence of events.

More importantly, in the search for the identity of the capturing submarine, Bill Armstrong of Nixa, MO, another reunion attendee, volunteered to research the submarine service records, a daunting and challenging task. Through tenacity and perseverance, he was able to achieve his objective. After months of research, he called to report his progress. He informed me he was close to identifying the capturing submarine and sent me pictures of the submarine tender, USS Fulton. It was anchored in Saipan Harbor with 13 submarines moored alongside.

He thought one of them maybe our target submarine. A short time later he called and informed me he had achieved his objective. The target submarine was moored alongside the USS Holland and the USS Baya. The name of the capturing submarine was the USS Becuna (SS31), whose captain was Commander Henry Dixon Sturr (now deceased). Lt. Commander Thomas Dabney was the Executive Officer and currently lives in St. Petersburg, FL.

Bill Armstrong phoned Lt. Comdr. Dabney and had an informative conversation and illumination, concerning both the executive officer and the USS Becuna. Lt. Commander Dabney is now 92 years old and is a 1936 graduate of the Naval Academy. He had retired after 30 years' service as a Captain.

The USS Becuna was on its maiden voyage when it left San Francisco, with a crew of 95, for Pearl Harbor. After refueling at Pearl Harbor, it continued onto Saipan and then on to Freemantle, Australia (Southwest coast near Perth.) This was his only voyage aboard the USS Becuna, because he was promoted on arrival in Australia and given command of his own submarine, the USS Quitarro. Two other submarines, the USS Baya and USS Hawkbill accompanied the USS Becuna on the trip.

It was on the Pearl Harbor to Saipan Harbor leg that the encounter with a small Japanese boat occurred. The Three submarines were in a column formation at 6-mile intervals. The USS Becuna was leading the formation, followed by the USS

Baya with the USS Hawkbill trailing. As the submarines were traveling on the surface, a visual contact was made with the Japanese boat

However, Lt. Comdr. Dabney said his memory of this event was vague so he would try to contact other members of the crew for their recollections. He could not recall the approximate location of the encounter, but would send Bill Armstrong a copy of the USS Becuna's deck log to document the capturing date and a picture of the officers.

The following September 1, 1944, the USS Becuna's deck log entry documented the capture of Cpl. Abe. 16-20 Underway as before, 16.51 all/ahead flank speed, changing course to 215 degree True per gyro compass; sighted small boat bearing 205 degrees true per gyro compass, slowed to standard speed 1700 maneuvering to go alongside boat and pick up the Japanese soldier. The soldier taken aboard as prisoner, then the 1735 commenced firing at the small boat with machine guns. At 1735 the boat deck was awash and sinking. 11750 changed course to 262 degrees true per gyrocompass, going ahead 16knots. 1830 resuming zigzagging, base course, 262 degrees true per gyrocompass.

By coincidence, I was in St. Petersburg soon after Bill Armstrong's call and knew exactly where Lt. Comdr. Dabney lived. I phoned and was invited to meet him at his home on Feb. 21, 2005. After my arrival, we conversed about the capture for over an hour and I took his picture. He informed me that he had been unsuccessful in making contact with any USS Becuna crewmembers. He said that the USS Becuna was decommissioned is 1967 and is now a museum in Philadelphia, Pa. He also said, if given time, he might be able to work out the approximate location for the encounter and would send me a copy of the USS Becuna's deck log for my review and Records. Again, all this information was a result of Bill Armstrong's research, as he successfully identified the capturing submarine as the USS Becuna.

They said the Captain of the submarine radioed Naval Authorities in Pearl Harbor on September 1st, 1944 that while on station, East of Guam, they sighted a small Japanese vessel, apparently used for recreational fishing, which was dead in the water. Since it was a great distance from land, he speculated it must have been blown out to sea by a recent storm and ran out of fuel. They captured the boat and aboard was a lone Japanese man, in uniform, about 30 years of age, who denied he understood English. The Captain was suspicious of the denial. American Naval Intelligence was interested in interrogating the prisoner and our ship was to bring him to Pearl Harbor.

I witnessed the prisoner's transfer to our ship in Saipan, from the starboard wing of the bridge and observed a small, uniformed, hatless man in handcuffs and loose leg irons, who seemed to be shaking with fright. The Captain issued orders, via the public address system, that the prisoner was not to be abused in any way. He was to remain in handcuffs, leg irons and be chained to a stanchion to prevent any attempt at suicide.

Two unarmed men were to guard him 24 hours a day. The prisoner quickly regained his composure, reinforcing the thought that he understood English. He was confined to a large area on the starboard side of the aft main deck. We left for Pearl Harbor on September 19, 1944. Initially, the Ship's Company considered him a great curiosity and attempted to communicate with him, but after a few days the novelty wore of.

A Chinese American crewman who spoke some Japanese attempted, on several occasions, to engage him in conversation, but he pretended he did not understand; however after a few days at sea the guards reported they were certain he understood English. He was brought to the fantail of the ship daily, because the weather was good and he became comfortable with his surroundings.

Visiting was permitted. My time with the prisoner was limited. I had no custodial duties or any other reason to visit him. My assignment was with a small group of technicians, involved in electronic detection of Japanese aircraft, ships and submarines, so I had little time or interest in visiting him. I saw him on the fantail from the bridge occasionally, but to me he was just a passenger held in restraint.

Our ship stopped at Eniwetok in the Marshall Islands to refuel, then continued on to Pearl Harbor. It was during this latter phase of the trip when word came to the bridge, that the prisoner finally admitted understanding English. Later that day, I went to his quarters and asked him to write his name on a "Hawaiian Invasion" dollar bill. He did as I had requested, but spoke no English. I am sure that other crewmen did the same. Later on I heard that he had been a student somewhere in the United States, but he never verified that. We arrived in Pearl Harbor on October 1st, 1944 and the prisoner was transferred to the Naval Authorities there.

Picture of Officers aboard the SS Becuna, in 1944

Japanese prisoners disembarking at Pearl Harbor 1944

Hawaiian Invasion Dollars, signed by Japanese prisoner, Cpl. Abe Tsuchimatsu

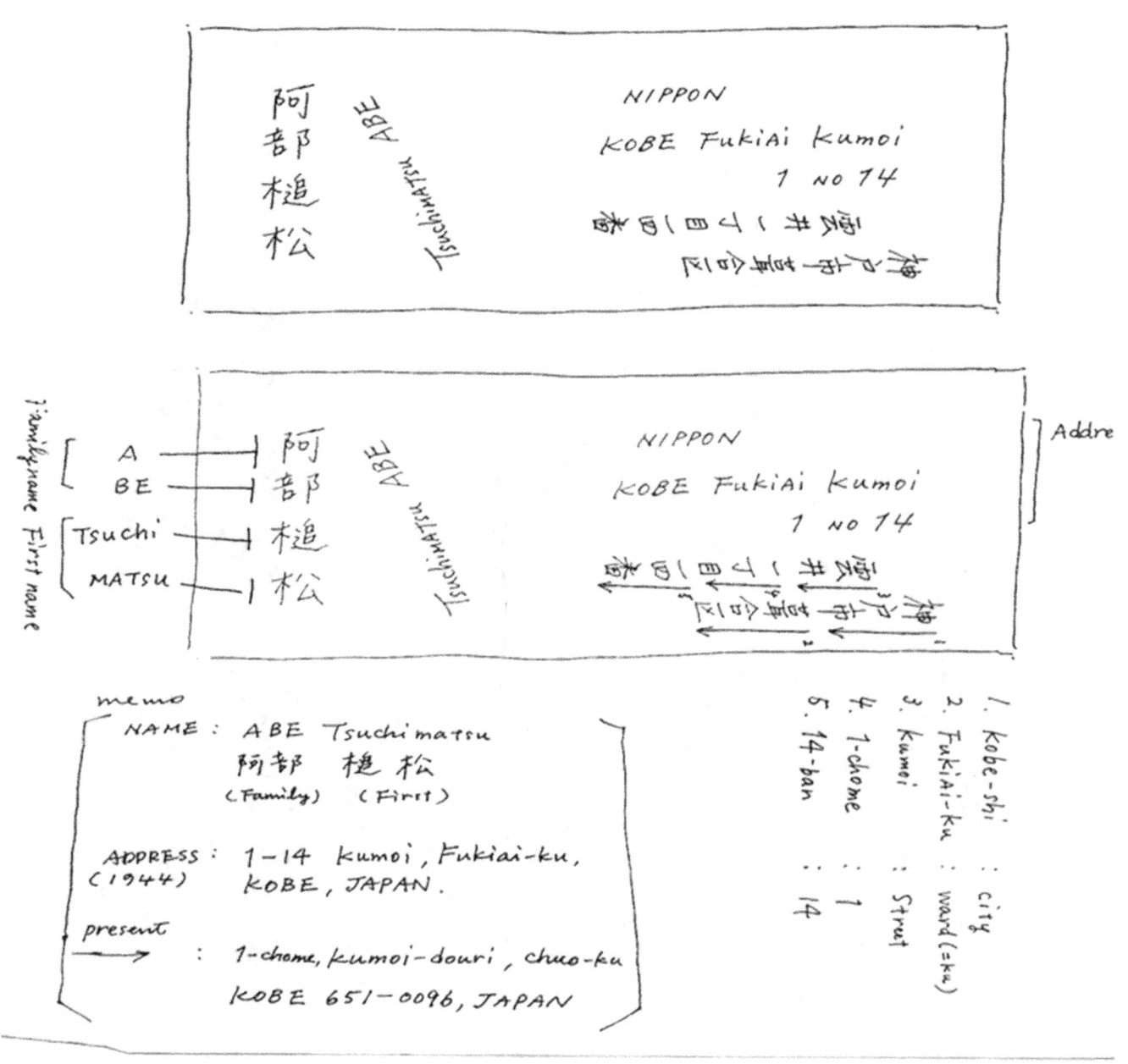

JAPANESE PRISONER ABE TSUCHIMATSU FAMILY ADDRESSES IN KOBE JAPAN

I RECEIVED THIS LETTER FROM THIS OFFICER JUST A FEW YEARS AGO IN 2007. HOW IRONIC WAS THE TIMING OF THIS LETTER, FOLLOWING THE ARRIVAL OF THE CHINCOTEAGUE AT PEARL HARBOR, TO DISCHARGE THE JAPANESE PRISONER. THIS LETTER FOLLOWS!

Wilderness canoe trips for boys
in the Province of Quebec
DIRECTORS AND WINTER ADDRESSES

Roderick Beebe, Jr.
The Gunnery School
Washington, Conn. 06793

Carl R. Williams
Salisbury School
Salisbury, Conn. 06068

Camp Kapitachouane

KAPITACHUAN CLUB, P.Q.
via SENNETERRE, P.Q.

4 April 2007

Mr.   Bill Armstrong
USS Chincoteague   AVP-24
101 Willow Lane
Nixa, MO 65714

Dear Bill:

It was good to talk with you on the phone about my brief experience
with the Chincoteague. My story goes like this:

I was the ASW officer aboard the USS Stafford, DE-411 in 1944. We
were in Pearl Harbor undergoing some boiler repairs in September-
October of 1944 (which was fortunate because it kept us out of our
assigned position in the screen of TAFFY Three in the Battle of
Leyte Gulf. Anyway, periodically we had to assign either officers
or men to the Honolulu Shore Patrol. My duty came up on October 2nd
as you can see from the enclosed log page. I reported to the SP
office with other officers and men from various ships for the day's
duty.   The O-in-C of the SP was a LCDR who had run a laundry in
Chicago and was a real SOB, according to rumors. When we were all
assembled, he addressed us and said "Each of you is getting a book
of 20 (maybe more?- I can't remember) report tickets and you are to
fill them all out or you will be called back for SP duty tomorrow
(which NOBODY wanted). You are to put people on report for ANY in-
fraction that you see; drunk and disorderly, failure to salute,cre-
ating a disturbance, etc. etc.You will each be assigned with a full
time regular duty Shore Patrol Member. So go out now and don't come
back until all those tickets are given out."

So thus began my one and only duty as a Shore Patrol officer.My
assigned SP member and I started out along the main drag in Honolulu
(I can't remember the name.- Maybe Queen St?) and looked for some
offenders. They were easy to find. I think that the Chincoteague
had just come in from SoPac and this was the first liberty for the
crew. The last thing those hardened sailors were interested in was
the saluting of some Ensign. So I got rid of my book of tickets

Camp Kapitachouane

*Wilderness canoe trips for boys
in the Province of Quebec*

DIRECTORS AND WINTER ADDRESSES

Roderick Beebe, Jr.
The Gunnery School
Washington, Conn. 06793

Carl H. Williams
Salisbury School
Salisbury, Conn. 06068

KAPITACHUAN CLUB, P.Q.
via SENNETERRE, P.Q.

quite quickly, most of them given out to enlisted men from the Chincoteague, for failure to salute an officer. The only other part of my SP duty that I remeber, is trying to keep an orderly line-up of customers outside a whorehouse!!! Anyway, when my tour was done, and my assistant and I were returning to the SP Base, I said to him, " I hope I never meet the Captain or any of the men from The Chincoteague. They'll kill me!"

So anyway, now the truth is finally out. I apologize to all the men of the Chincoteague and I hope you have a wonderful reunion. All the best.

Sincerely,

Carl H. Williams

USS BECUNA (SS-31) WW II

Here is a follow up, regarding the Japanese prisoner of war information. In my research and also with more information, supplied by Walter Jagger, I contacted one of my cousins, living in California, who for several years had been a teacher in Japan. He had become interested in the story and had forwarded this information to his fiancée, who was Japanese, and presently living there. She became quite excited, regarding this story, after receiving the information describing the general area his family had been living and sadly reported that the area in Kobe, Japan, listed as the family home address had been totally destroyed, from the bombings during the war years in WW II, everyone was saddened by this information, but this wouldn't become the only sad ending from the events of WW II.

Billie R. Armstrong

JOHN E. DAVIS, SOM1/C USS CHINCOTEAGUE AVP-24 OCTOBER 1944-MAY 1946

Based in a barracks on Ford Island and on a beer delivering working party, in early in Oct, 1944. When we finished late that afternoon, I checked the Draft Board, as we were told to do every day, and finally had a ship. It was the USS Chincoteague, but it was in dry-docking for overhaul. I was instructed to report immediately for a physical so, as dirty as I was and probably smelling a little like the beer we had been delivering all day, I reported as ordered. The pharmacist mate said he was going to put me on report if didn't clean up a little. CAN'T Win!!

I Reported aboard the Chincoteague that night and was assigned quarters with my Division, so I began meeting shipmates. Second morning, new blood! I caught my first "working party" aboard ship. The party was to chip and red lead the voids in the cofferdam. I found out I definitely did not become claustrophobic.

The ship made several trips to Maui and other islands for a shakedown. We loaded supplies and ammunition and prepared to shove off. The wharf was crowded with people to see us off, so the skipper decided to give them a show. He backed her away smartly, but one of the hawsers became tangled in one of the screws. The Capt. never slowed down to indicate that there was a problem, so we cruised out of Pearl on one screw. When we were outside the harbor and out of sight, divers cleared the screw and we were underway.

CHINCOTEAGUE, CREWMEMBERS HAVING A BEER BRAKE ON ULITHI MOG MOG, ISLAND 1944

A short stop was made in Eniwetok Atoll and then on to Ulithi. This anchorage was still being used with large groups of Carriers, Battleships, Cruisers and all the support groups stopping off for a few days, before continuing west. I could identify with Mr. Roberts in the play and the movie "Mr. Roberts" when he gazed upon this large massive battle fleet gathering and awaking one morning to find they had departed. Ulithi had the famous Mog Mog Island for recreation parties, two beers (or cokes) and a few hours under a Coconut tree. The West Virginia was in port, so I contacted a high school buddy and we were able to visit for a short period. I decided to try and meet the next day on Mog Mog, if possible. We did find each other on the island and he had brought me a number of copies of the hometown paper.

Kossel Passage or Kossol Roads was the Chincoteague's destination, in early Dec. of 1944. This was the fleet's anchorage on the northern end of the Palau Islands. It is an extensive natural anchorage and lies off the by-passed island of Babelthaup. The invasion of Peleliu was in progress at this time. The Chincoteague went from Kossol Roads to Peleliu to start operations, during the invasion. The Chincoteague had a squadron of Black Cats in Peleliu. One of the Black Cats had to make an emergency landing and ended up near the enemy's beach on Babeltaup Island. Under the cover of darkness, the Chincoteague moved as close to the beach as possible, lowered a motor whaleboat and took a line to the plane.

The ship was at battle stations, since Babelthaup was said to have several thousand japs on it and we were expecting to come under attack. Needless to say, the Black's crews were sure glad to see us. The plane was slowly towed away from the beach and tied to the Chincoteague. The plan was to save the plane, but the ocean towage was too rough, so the plane was stripped and sunk. There was a fringe reef around part of the anchorage at Peleliu.

This reef was, at times, only about knee deep and the Japs used it at night, in the early days of the invasion, to try and infiltrate marine positions. Scuttlebutt had it that the Japs were swimming out to the ships off the shallow reef, slipping silently aboard in the darkness and knifing crewmembers. Sailors were making request from family and friends to send them combat knifes. Many were received, so you would always shake your watch relief very gently and stand clear.

The Chincoteague went back to Kossol Roads to tend planes and be on standby for-air-sea rescue. There was no place to get off the ship for recreation in this large anchorage, so large rafts were built for swimming and recreation. One day about midmorning, the anchorage erupted in all kinds of noise and confusion. A Jap mini-sub had gotten into the anchorage.

Anti-submarines were trying to get underway to combat the sub, but small craft were going in every direction and sonar would not work, with all the many steel hulled craft present. The anchorage Commander was trying for radio silence so an attack could be organized, but to no avail. The Jap finally rammed a small tanker and they located him so the sub, in turn was also rammed. It was wild for a while!

As a seaplane tender, we would be anchored in one place for weeks and weeks. The mid-watch was always monotonous when you are not underway. My watch/battle station was in CIC (Combat Information Center) and in the radar compartment we had a coffee pot and hot plate. When on mid-watch, one of us would go by the bakery and pick up a warm loaf of bread that had been freshly baked. An onion would have been picked up from the spud locker and then we'd slip (I hate to say steal) a can of Spam from the lifeboat rations.

Warm Spam-onion sandwiches seemed to make the watch go better. The Life Boat Inspectors raised hell, and rightly so, but the Spam was replaced only to disappear again. My family gives me a bad time, but I still love a Spam sandwich. About 22:30 one evening (10:30PM), The Chincoteague was ordered to get underway to conduct a search for a B-25 and three crewmembers that were missing, following a bombing mission in the Philippines. The Capt. was attending a party aboard another ship, so they had to bring him back aboard with the aid of lots of Black, Hot Coffee. We not only prepared to get underway, but also went to General Quarters. The Capt. took us out through a narrow reef channel at flank speed, using searchlights and sonar to try and keep us off the reef. The Chincoteague was in position by daylight and we started a grid search. We knew that we were in the right place, because floating landing gear and other debris were sighted. It was an all-day search with the entire crew manning the rails. The search was about to be terminated when one of the airmen was spotted. He was hanging on to a pillow-sized air packet in a deflated life raft. I was on the signal-bridge rail and could see there were at least a dozen sharks swimming around him and tugging at the raft.

The Capt. Yelled down to the foc'sle and said, "Take that man a line" and without hesitation, the Chief Bosun Mate dove into the sea with a line. I thought that was as brave an act as I had ever witnessed. It was something to see and remember. The airman was pulled aboard and after he was revived, he said that we had passed him three times that day. No sign of his buddies, that's a big old ocean!! Incidentally, the sharks pulled the raft completely under when it was abandoned.

Jose Perez, above left, walks the streets of Honolulu.

ANOTHER MEMORY OF THIS RESCUE BY LT. JOSE PEREZ

USS Chincoteague (AVP-24) was a destroyer-sized seaplanes tender, the length of a football field, but much broader abeam, than a destroyer. AVPs function was used as hotels, restaurants, gas stations garages, medical clinics and movie theatres, for assigned seaplane squadrons.

The Chincoteague, operating independently in the Southwest Pacific in 1944, received orders to proceed to Peleliu Island, in the Palau Island group, to assume air-sea rescue duties. The Palau's are approximately 500 miles east of the Philippines and 1,000 miles west of the neutralized Japan Bastion at Truk AVPs, the "mother hens" to seaplanes squadrons. They perform yeoman services in patrolling war zones. The stubby little ships also tended PT-boat squadrons. The AVPs broad beam gave the ship extra space to accommodate squadrons crews for extensive periods of operation.

It also had enough space astern to lift a plane aboard for repair and maintenance. Upon arrival, we found Peleliu still occupied by remnants of the Japanese army. The 1st Marine division under famed Lewis B. (Chesty) Puller, then a Lieutenant Colonel, had invaded Peleliu to capture the airfield on its southern tip. It was the largest Japanese air base in the Palau's and was needed to establish a bomber base for the U.S. Army Air Forces that were used in the Philippine campaign. The Army's 81st Infantry Regiment had attacked Angaur Island 10 miles south of Peleliu, without much resistance.

It later rendered assistance to the Peleliu battle by first sending in its 321st and 323rd combat teams. The resistance on Peleliu was much greater than expected; the battle wore on to become one of the bloodiest island-hopping campaign's in the pacific war. We dropped anchor near the base in a coral-protected area by Kossel Roads, which was used as a small fleet anchorage. B-29 bombers were making daily sorties on the Philippine's in preparation for the invasion and General Douglas MacArthur's triumphant return.

Mid-morning, three days after our arrival, a message came in announcing that a U.S. bomber had gone down, upon its return to the Peleliu base. Immediately, we upped anchor and moved slowly out of the bay, picked up speed and began the search. We patrolled all day without success, continuing to search after sunset. We steamed to the other side of the island to take advantage of a full moon. Japanese searchlights pierced the darkness as they beamed back and forth, but they did not sweep low enough to spot the ship. Luck did not come our way that night and we returned to Kossel Roads.

At dawn the next day, we continued the search, with the help of a small Piper-sized Army aircraft. It is extremely difficult to spot an object in the choppy waters of a vast ocean from the bridge of a ship. Nevertheless, at about noon, the ship's pilot spotted a man hugging a deflated yellow life raft kept buoyant by what we later learned, was a well-packed radio. We sped to the location and then moved slowly to within 30 yards of the raft. Over the side went a cargo net. Into the water dove the Chief boatswain's mate. At the same time, sailors manning the ship's bow, fired rifles to ward off the sharks circling the life raft.

The boatswain's mates' only thought, as he dove into the ocean, was of a quick rescue. He was oblivious to shark-infested waters and moved with the speed of an Olympic swimmer. He grabbed the man and hauled him to the cargo net. Both were pulled aboard by an anxious crew. The moment the man was safe on deck, in the arms of his savior, he collapsed into unconsciousness. Certainly, the airman's persistence was proof of the axiom, "airman's fight for survival brings forth unbelievable strengths."

The Chincoteague was released from its'Kossol duty and we headed for Saipan to pick up fresh supplies. A small working party was formed on Sunday morning with an (LCI Landing Craft Infantry), to receive the stores. They tied up to the Merchantman to take on the new stores, but the Merchant Marines would not load the stores, because it was Sunday and they didn't work on Sunday's. We knew that we were headed for an Invasion somewhere, but the fighting almost started a little early that morning. The LCI finally returned to the ship and picked up a full working party to load the supplies.

We left Saipan and arrived at the Island of Guam, tying up alongside a troop transport. The Poor, ole "Jar Heads" had been on the transport nearly a month. They would line the rail all day long when possible to visit, and at night would watch the movie we were showing on the fantail. I've often wondered how many of them were watching their last movie on those nights. A new high powered- Smoke Generator was installed between the depth charge racks on the Chincoteague's fantail. The Chincoteague got underway Feb. 15 and joined a taskforce for the invasion of Iwo Jima. Our assignment was on the port bow of the troop transports. The invasion fleet arrived at Iwo, the 18th of Feb. and the invasion started early the morning of February the 19th. The Jap bombers attacked late that afternoon and into the evening hours, but that was the last encounter with the Japanese Air Forces.

The Chincoteague was ordered to "Make Smoke-Make Smoke". With our new smoke generator, we really covered our portion of the task force. I've thought many times since then about other ships, which were well covered, but they were steaming on the edge of the fleet at full speed and uncovered with smoke streaming out of the fantail? Who else? "The Chincoteague". The Chincoteague was anchored about 200 yards offshore and directly under Mt.Suribachi. Seaplane Operations were setup the second morning, following the invasion.

The Ship drew a sporadic amount of fire from the mountain, until they eventually recognized we were waiting for them to help pinpoint our fire. Feb.23 dawned and this would be the first day to see a bright sunlight filled sky since arriving at Iwo Jima. About mid-morning, every horn, whistle or noise maker sounded in the anchorage. This was the noisiest day we had heard since our arrival at the Island. Everyone came to attention, trying to decide just what was happening. When when we looked above the Chincoteague, there on the top of Mt, Suribachi, "Old Glory" was waving in all its beauty, and splendor. I don't believe I've ever felt a stronger feeling and, even today, I can tear-up thinking of that moment when we saw the flag.

The water was extremely rough and the pilots were having trouble. JATO "Jet Assisted Takeoff" was introduced to us for the first time. This device was attached to each side of the aircraft and when more speed was needed to get your plane airborne, the jets were kicked in to assist and they really did the job, fast and effective. One sight we could see on the Beach was a Sea-Bee or Marine Operator on his dozer cutting a switch-back road up Suribachi. We could tell from the smoke that the fighting was still in progress. He seemed just as calm as could be and it actually looked like he had a cigar in his mouth, as he continued pushing dirt off the side of the road, (That was real John Wayne stuff).

The Invasion of Iwo Jima, February 19, 1945

The invasion of Iwo Jima, February 19 1945 The Chincoteague was ahead in the distance

Seaplane landing at Iwo Jima, February, 1945

The Chincoteague's radar was used to guide the first damaged B-29 to make an emergency landing on the Island. After they had issued a "Mayday" call for support, saying that they were going to have to ditch, so as a result, with the help of our radar assistance, they were directed to the Island and landed on the field. With fighting still in progress on the one end, what must the Jap's have thought when they observed this enormous aircraft land? March 10, the Airfield on the Island had been secured and as the Chincoteague's Aircraft were no longer needed, we left the Marines to continue to deal with the death and carnage on Iwo Jima. We had only four casualties aboard the Chincoteague, which occurred on the first nights air raid from friendly fire. A Gun tub on the signal bridge was hit by what, inspection determined, must have resulted from a 40mm-AA projectile, during one of the Air raids.

The Chincoteague, departed Iwo Jima, arriving at Guam on March 13 and Saipan on 16, where supplies were beginning to stack up for the coming invasion of Japan. We observed a huge endless line of supplies and equipment. One year later, we were again witnesses to this huge store of supplies, that we had observed before in Saipan. I understand that the cost was too high to try and return, and the material that was not bought for salvage was left to rot!

Seaplane Operations were commenced again in Ulithi. This anchorage had been left somewhat in the rears of the conflict, because operations had move on and this area was bypassed; however we did observe the casualties from the war in Okinawa while passing, such as the Carrier Franklin. It was such a burned out hull that I was surprised to see it was being towed back to Pearl Harbor.

The Chincoteague was finally ordered home, so we left Pearl Harbor on June 21 and arrived in San Pedro, CA-USA- June 29, via San Diego. The Chincoteague was there, in the process of being overhauled, when the war ended. We all were given leave, which would be my first one. There had been no "Boot Camp leave", due to my sonar class starting a week after finishing and when that schooling was finished, I was shipped out right away.

Day, the war was over!

I had liberty that day, so Walt Jagger and I decided to travel to Los Angeles. The city was a madhouse and the streets were full with everyone dancing and yelling. It seemed that ever third person wanted to have a drink with a service man. Walt and I tried to hold up the traditions of a sailor, but by 8:30 or 9:00 that night, we had a little trouble getting each other back to the ship. We made it back aboard the Chincoteague, and into our bunks. (I think.)

The Chincoteague left San Diego, in the middle of September and we knew from the new shots, that we were headed to the Far East. The replacements, mostly from Louisiana and S. Texas, seemed to have an extra rough time with seasickness on the way to Pearl Harbor, but soon settled into the routine. It was a strange feeling being underway, with the Guns covered and seeing smoking topsides at night. The drills didn't stop though, with General Quarters at dawn, Gun Drills thru the day, a fire drill, and abandon ship every once in a while.

We left Pearl Harbor, the first week in October, headed for Okinawa, by way of Midway. We arrived in Buckner Bay, Okinawa, on the 30th of October. The Chincoteague had just missed one of the worse typhoons that Okinawa had ever experienced and that was evident. Large Ships and many Landing Craft littered the beach, having been blown out of the water. The Chincoteague left for Tsingtao, China, the first week in November and sailed alertly through the heavily mined Yellow Sea. We blew up two floating Mines with 20mm Cannons and didn't have too much trouble keeping plenty of people on watch.

The aftermath from the Typhoon at the Island of Okinawa, October, 1946

The Yellow Sea was also full of Giant Jelly–fish (Man-of-War) the size of a large washtub, which is one of the reasons pilots were so leery about having to ditch in those waters. Tsingtao, China was an old city, (Everything in China was old) with a large Cathedral and a few Business Buildings.

The Liberty Pier extended probably two city blocks into the Bay, due to high and low tides. The Harbor is a large exposed body of water subject to very strong windstorms. During one of those storms, we had to get underway to hold our position in the Harbor. Every ship in the harbor was dragging its' anchor. The storm caught us by surprise and sank the Captains' Gig and a Motor Whale-boat, which was tied to a boom alongside. It was one of the coldest places I've ever seen. We were issued marine winter gear (long socks, combat boots, jackets and etc.), because the ship could not stay heated. How cold was it? They usually mustered Divisions, one at a time, on the Fantail for "short-arm" inspection, but there were too many layers of clothes or it was just too cold for exposure, so it was moved below.

The Louisiana and South Texas replacements saw the first snow of their lives and you would have thought we had a bunch of 10 year olds at Disney Land. I have experienced that type of cold weather one other time. The small Carrier I was on during the Korean War was operating off Vladivostok, Russia, when our Marine Squadron was trying to help evacuate the Marines out of the Chosin, Reservoir area. We were using the entire crew to clear the Flight- Deck of Ice and Snow, so those crazy guys could continue to land and takeoff. (But that is another story).

I had an Aunt in Childress, Texas that sent me a clipping and pictures from the front page of the local paper, which showed the Crew trying to clear the Flight-Deck of Snow and Ice. It surprised us to see that someone, other than families, were aware of activities over there.

Sailor taking a ride in a Rickshaw, Tsingtao, China 1946

Pagoda Pier, Tsingtao, China

Back to Tsingtao, one of our entertainments on the beach (which we realize now was very (Ugly AMERICAN) was racing with rickshaws, making the Chinamen ride, while we would do the pulling and racing. There was much shouting, wrecks and torn blues.

Liberty In Tsingtao, China

It was downhill to the Liberty Pier, so the havoc was caused on our way back to the Ship. There was a small café that served steak and eggs. We could hardly wait to have those fresh eggs and that good ground steak. That's another thing I've thought about through the years, I had never seen a Cow or Calf in China and I just wondered what that ground beef could have been.

USS Chincoteague Feb. 25 1946 Whanpoo River Shanghai China

We were the last to take on refugees and leave Tsingtao, as you could hear the Communist guns outside the city. We arrived in Shanghai the last week in February and set-up Seaplane Operations. It was about the same as Tsinghai, except more of the same; old, dirty and millions of Chinese. We had to patrol the plane anchorage to try and keep the thieves away from the planes.

This worked for a while, but they found a way to slip into the planes, so the crews started staying in the planes. This worked for a while, until the enterprising Chinese found they could take girls out to the planes for parties. Then it really hit the fan from the Chinese side and the Capt.'s.

It was a continuous problem and even with armed patrolling it would just be cat and mouse with the Chinese. The orders came for us to return to the Gulf Coast in the States. The Capt. arranged for us to return through the Indian Ocean, Suez, Mediterranean, and home across the Atlantic. We were ready to sail when our orders were cancelled. The crew was frozen in the service and we were to report to Bikini

Atoll for the Hydrogen Bomb testing. With the change of orders, and low morale, we set sail from Shanghai, the last week in February for Saipan.

Provisions were loaded in Saipan and the Chincoteague headed for Bikini Atoll, to set up Seaplane Operations. A typhoon fury intensified, changing course and caught the Chincoteague. There was no way to dodge or skirt the storm, so the Chincoteague just tried to keep the bow heading directly into the wind. A few degrees off would have rolled us over for sure. That may have been what happened to the Destroyers that were lost in the Philippines and Okinawa storms. For two days, the Chincoteague may as well been a Submarine, as most of the time we were completely immersed and the screws would come completely out of the water.

Cold cuts and coffee were available for those that could eat or drink, but it was impossible to get braced enough to stay in your bunk. There was a man on the helm with a standby, as it was a constant battle to keep the bow in a straight heading into the wind. I had been aboard over a year and this was my first time to use "Officers-Country" as a passenger to and from the Bridge, because no one could get out on the deck. The Chincoteague was badly damaged, but once again, "IT WAS THE SHIP THAT WOULDN'T SINK." The damage was bad enough to have our orders cancelled for the Bikini Operation and to be ordered back to the States!

The Chincoteague sailed home by the way of Midway, Pearl Harbor, and San Diego in the middle of April. The Ship was repaired enough to sail down the Coast, through the Panama Canal and arrive in New Orleans, May 2, 1946. I was aboard three more weeks, as plans were being made to decommission the Chincoteague. Personnel were leaving so fast for separation that it became evident that the Crew was too short to sail to Orange, Texas for decommission.

The solution to that on the Chincoteague, and I'm sure other ships, was to offer advancement in rank, if you would sign over for another 3 years. It was strange, but I know of no takers for this program. We all had our "What if's---and I have thought many times, wouldn't a 20-year-old CPO go over big in the Chief's quarters"? If it had happened, I would have had my 20 in and been 38 years old, and too, it sure would have made a difference if I had been called back as a Chief in 1950. The Chief's aboard a Carrier did live really well!!

John E. Davis SOG I/C-375-55-09

"Bridge Gang"

Chow Down! Let's Eat!

The Deck Gang Group

Ships Defensive Crews: (Gun & Ammunition & etc.)

Commander Rosasco cuts the Chincoteague's Second birthday Cake, September 1945

Captain R. A. Rosasco, The Second Commander Of The USS Chincoteague

This chapter I try showing contrast in leadership between two Commanding Officers that had graced the bridge of the USS Chincoteague. They were both graduates of the Naval Academy, but that is where the story differs as to character, Hobbs, stern in manner, somewhat aloof in nature, detached somewhat, from my prospective. Captain R.A. Rosasco was his opposite in nature.

My own experiences were somewhat of a different nature. I will describe. During the time period, our ship was in Dry-dock at Mare Island Naval Repair Facility, having repairs made for the battle damage, it was the policy while welders were doing this process, and shipmates had to provide fire protection to prevent an accidental fire. We had to provide this 24 hours of protection in 4-hour sequences. This meant that during the week each of those non-rated crew-members could expect at least two sessions of this duty.

As an 18 year old kid, I had made friends with another one of the crew aboard the Chincoteague, who informed me he was about to depart on leave, within a few days to his home, either in Utah or Wyoming. The destination is not very clear at this time, late in life. This had me very excited, wishing to join him on his trip, but the problem was that I didn't have leave time available for me, but maybe I could find a solution and could join him.

Now at 18 years of age, logic doesn't play a dominant role in the thinking process, so I asked Chief Culpepper, of my division, if it were possible for me to acquire the following Monday off, and find a person to stand my Friday fire watch. He said he would ask the division Officer about the extra day. The next afternoon I was told that my request had been granted. I had also found another crew-member who agreed (for ten dollars) he would do my fire-watch. So that Friday afternoon off we went, hitch-hiking, across the country.

We arrived in Salt Lake City, late Saturday afternoon. We stepped from the car; that had given us our last lift, and began walking along the street. After about 10 minutes, a Highway Patrol car slowed down beside us, asking "where you Sailors heading"? We told him our destination then he asked for our leave papers, which my friend supplied. He then turned to me and asked for mine. I replied that I had none, but that I had Liberty until the following Tuesday.

His reply was this: "you're outside your Naval District and you need leave papers, so then he instructed me to step inside the Patrol car, because I was under Arrest! My shipmate continued on his journey. I went to the County Jail. To shorten the story, I would spend the next two weeks in this County Resort. I had not been given the opportunity to take a shower, during my stay at this bug infested joint, only the use of the sink for that purpose. I didn't have a change of clothes and would wash my under garments at night and sleep in the nude.

I became very ill and was transported to a Military facility hospital. I had some form of poisoning, due to the swarms of bedbugs that infested the jail cells. After a few days, I was informed that a Sailor had arrived to transport me back to California and that the money for this transportation would be taken from my pay.

We returned by train; arriving at Mare Island and the Ship again. I was locked in the Marine Brig there. After a few days, I was presented at the Capitan's Mast and met our new Commanding Officer, Rosasco. He read the charges against me and asked why I had taken this trip, without obtaining approved Leave Papers. I explained that I was not aware it was illegal to leave the State; saying that the division Chief Culpepper knew my destination and had not informed me that this would require Leave Papers. I had planned for my return on time, had I not been in Jail. I was also told that my Fire-watch had not been filled. I informed him that I had paid a Ship-mate 10 dollars to fill in for me.

His decision was 30 days restriction, no liberty, saying," You have spent enough time locked up". This doesn't end my story; I returned to the barracks, and after

Captains' Mast, I confronted the Ship-mate that I had given the 10 dollars to fill my spot. I really laid a good punch on him!

He had taken the money that night to San Francisco. He was back again, before Capt. Rasasco could give him 30 days restriction. Two weeks later I was called before Capt. Rasasco. He privately stated: "You've had enough punishment, the remaining restrictions are removed"!

Daniel Bryan, later to become a Radioman in rating, would at first become the pilot of the Captains Gig that would transport Captain Rosasco to and from his varied locations, when at anchor.

Rosasco had become an avid snorkel diver whenever the ship was anchored at any new anchorage and would spend many hours away from the ship performing his passion, with Daniel Bryan as his Gig driver, he'd go wherever the Captains whims directed. He loved to explore the many reef structures at different harbors that became part of their agenda. During the ships deployment in the Marshall Islands, Eniwetok Atoll, in 1944, the Captain decided to again explore one of the coral reefs that encompassed the island. Gathering his scuba gear, he directed Bryan to transport him across the harbor, some distance away from the ship, where he descended into the depths. At a point, some fifteen minutes later, an air raid alarm sounded at the anchorage.

Bryan, seeing the need to contact the Captain, dove into the water to alert him of this warning. He descended to about 20 feet, saw Captain Rosasco and tapped him on the shoulder to gain his attention. Suddenly, the Captain reacted with a knife in hand, just missing Bryan in a sudden thrust. Bayan pointed upward, toward the surface, in a wild gesture; then they ascended to the surface making a fast retreat back to the ship.

Rosasco also liked his liquor and ladies and when the ship happened to be at anchor, near any large facility with a hospital, which employed female nurses, he made sure that much of his leisure evenings would be spent ashore where ladies had residence, enjoying their company, along with free flowing of spirits. He would return back to the ship in the wee hours of the morning. On several occasions he had been observed returning aboard ship with a female friend in tow; also sometimes with more than one being chaperoned aboard.

On one such late evening he was returning to the ship just as the Captains Launch approached the gangway landing. He stepped from the Launch as a slight surge occurred and into the drink, plunged the skipper; after some few minutes he was pulled aboard the landing, and then someone dove back into the ocean to retrieve his Cap. On another venture, Bryan was assigned to retrieve a couple of the ships' Officers from some festivities ashore. He arrived to escort them back to the ship and Bryan remarked that it was apparent that both Officers had become well intoxicated during their visit. This was quite apparent as they fumbled, stumbling aboard the Captains Gig.

At almost the moment they came aboard, it was very easy to see that they were embroiled in some sort of disagreement as they shouted at each other. Suddenly, the larger of the two shoved the smaller one over the side, so Bryan slowed down the Gig. He was attempting to help bring the fellow aboard, but the stronger guy kept pushing him under. Bryan could tell the one in the water was losing his strength and decided to intervene. He shoved the one Officer aside while helping the other back in the boat. He finally arrived back at the Chincoteague and unloaded both drunken Officers aboard the ship.

The next day, Bryan was informed that both Officers had filed complaints against him for striking an Officer. This was a very serious charge; if he was convicted it meant many years in the Brig. Both Officers kept inquiring to Captain Rosasco as to when Bryan would be held accountable and tried for the offenses; finally, with Christmas approaching, he dismissed all charges against any person awaiting Captains Mast, on any charge. It was a Christmas Present for all!

Chincoteague on the Reef, Funafuti Atoll, April 9th, 1944

Sunday, April 9th, 1944, Funafuti Atoll and Ellice Islands Group were preparing for departure at 4:55-PM. They were to enter Teava Fuega Channel, at standard speed, 15 knots at 5: 03.

5:07-PM. Full speed ahead, but at 5:17PM, all engines slowed to 2/3speed. At 5:26PM the ship was aground on a soft coral ledge.

Here's a comment from Phillip Margetts, a QM3/C, aboard the Chincoteague, during that period.

I was a QM3/C at the time of the grounding; my duties were to go to the signal bridge to make sure we had the proper flags to display when entering port. Like if an Admiral was aboard or any other dignitary in port, who might be boarding. I would receive a light signal message from the port authority, asking for an ID; when confirmed, they would send back a berth number and any other information for the pilot.

The pilot would usually be aboard a pilot motor launch, a mile or so from the channel entrance. As soon as he came aboard, I was to raise his pilot flag showing he was in command. I raised the red flag, showing we had explosives aboard and the ID number to see before boarding. After completing that I went forward, looking for the pilots that were supposed to be just to the starboard of the ship's bow.

As soon as I approached the ships railing, I viewed the reef dead ahead and leaned over shouting! "Reef Dead Ahead" I am not sure if anyone had heard my shouted warning, because the ship continued on in a direct path toward the reef. I was not aware of any change of direction, nor did I observe the pilot. Apparently Capt. Rosasco decided he did not need a pilot, so he was proceeding on his own to enter the channel. As soon as everything quieted down, the Officer of the deck had me raise the grounding flag.

I then left the bridge area for other duties. 5:37PM. I began moving ammunition back aft to the stern of the ship, from the forward magazines (ammunition storage bunkers). I tried moving the ship off the reef using full engines in reverse. It was unsuccessful, so I began passing stern lines to PT Boats for towlines, again using full power in reverse, without any luck.

We started discharging diesel fuel, to lighten the ship. At 6:55PM, Boats from the beach were brought alongside and we started loading all Bombs, Ammunition and all topside gear into the Boats, so that all compartments remained dry. All hands continued unloading Bombs, ammunition and cargo. 9:59PM. Attempts continue with towlines from the tugs to pull the Chincoteague from the reef. At 11:04PM, the Commanding Officer orders that all tow lines be castoff and returned to their anchorages.

At 11:45PM, Capt. Rasasco orders all but 1,000 gallons of fuel oil dumped over the side. Monday 10th of April, 1944, efforts continue, removing approximately 378 tons. 133 lbs. of ammunition, 145lbs of oil and of misc. stores and deck gear. A new effort was started to finally remove the Chincoteague from its perch on the reef. At this juncture, it was decided to use another ship, the DE-32 Jenkins, along with a LSD-additionally. The ship would include the firing of its large 5'' 38'th's, in unison with the towing efforts from the added ships, could have a positive results. With an all-out effort it began, and finally at 5:59AM she was at last free.

At 7:55 Am, the USS Fleming came alongside our starboard quarter and the ships personnel returned aboard.

This picture was taken from the USS Chincoteague. The USS Fleming is in the background April 10, 1944

USS Fleming DE-32 1944

Daniel Bryan had, in one of our conversations regarding Capt. Rasasco, from a source he doesn't recall exactly who said and it related to Rasasco's demise. Following the ending of WW II, Rasasco had become the Commanding Officer on some small air station, somewhere within our Country. During a Saturday inspection on the airstrip, he drove up, stepped out onto the tarmac, walked a few steps and suddenly, collapsed with a heart attack. He was dead on the spot!

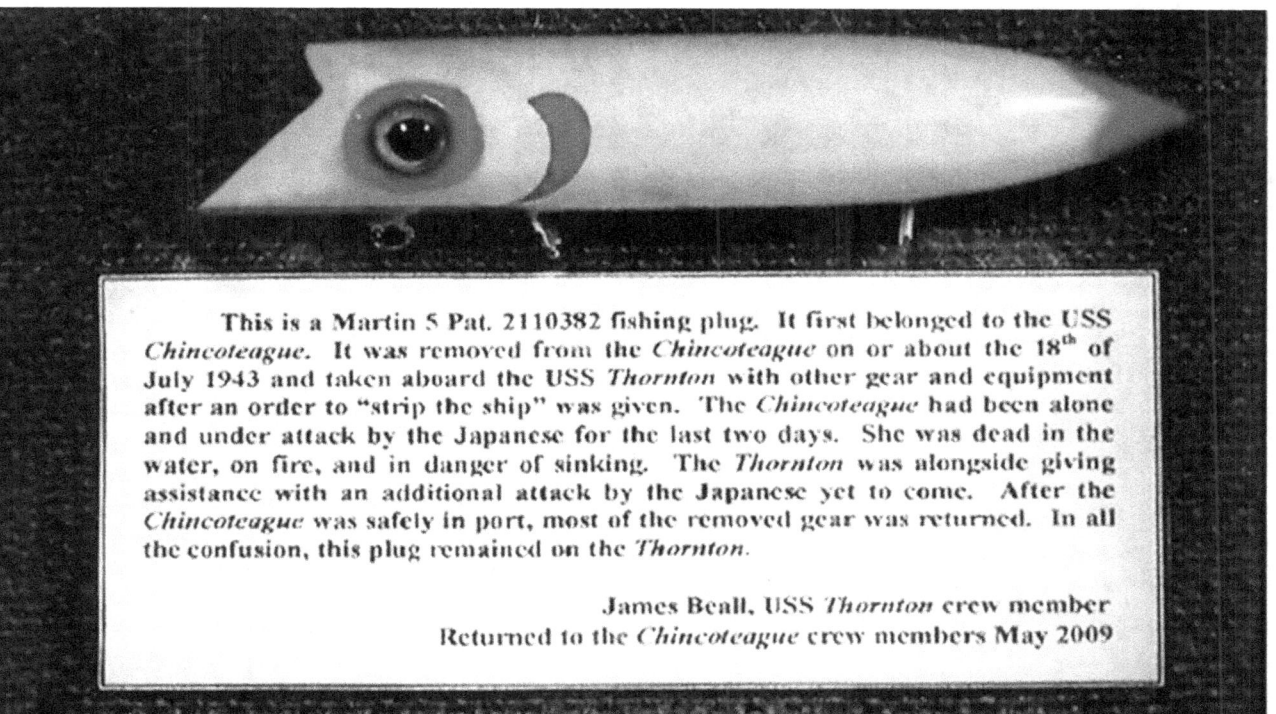

This is a Martin 5 Pat. 2110382 fishing plug. It first belonged to the USS *Chincoteague*. It was removed from the *Chincoteague* on or about the 18th of July 1943 and taken aboard the USS *Thornton* with other gear and equipment after an order to "strip the ship" was given. The *Chincoteague* had been alone and under attack by the Japanese for the last two days. She was dead in the water, on fire, and in danger of sinking. The *Thornton* was alongside giving assistance with an additional attack by the Japanese yet to come. After the *Chincoteague* was safely in port, most of the removed gear was returned. In all the confusion, this plug remained on the *Thornton*.

James Beall, USS *Thornton* crew member
Returned to the *Chincoteague* crew members May 2009

Bill Armstrong & Eddie Foster /1944Roi Namur Islands

Bill Armstrong & Eddie Foster, Roi Namur Islands Kwajalein Atoll 1944

A friend I had almost forgotten, Eddie Foster!

Looking back over the last sixty-eight years, when Eddie and I first became acquainted on the islands of Roi-Namur in the Marshall Islands, while members' of

CASU-F-20 (Carrier Aircraft Service Unit), I had been part of the Invasion Forces that had laid siege to this Island group, in early February 1944. I would return later that year in October, as a replacement person for those that had been part of the original CASU group. It was there that I first became acquainted with Eddie Foster; he was a Baker, and I a Cook. He had originally been assigned to CASU-F-30, during the occupation of Majuro, Atoll, some 400 miles south east of this Island group that we were now part of.

In a period of time, after becoming a member of the (Galley Gang), I was assigned as the Night Cook. My duties were to prepare the many items that would be part of the next day's meals (Breakfast, Lunch and Dinner items). My hours would start at about 6:00PM to12:00, AM-Eddy, from 12: 00, AM-7:00AM. We just became almost like brothers, spending much of our leisure hours together, walking on the reef. We hunted many varieties of shell creatures that were a part of this environment.

This Island location had no vegetation, or trees, because during the bombarding process they had destroyed any and all living trees, and plants. It was just a flat shade less blazing hot, flat white coral speck, just a few feet above surrounding ocean, roasting in the middle of the South-Pacific. When the wind was blowing, this was quiet a pleasant environment, but during those periods when it was calm, it could be a roaster on your body.

It was a nightmare cooking in the daytime environment; a corrugated steel nightmare. It was just a Quonset hut building, with no ventilation where, during the days working temperatures it could exceed 1:35 degrees inside. Eddies previous location Majuro atoll, was a contrast; I believe this was the only Japanese occupied location that evacuated prior to an invasion, without a shot fired. It makes you wonder what the reason was. A possibility may have been the location, which was many hundreds of miles removed from any of their other occupied areas. This would make it almost impossible to receive any aid or supplies. Anyway, this was what many would call your tropical paradise; palm trees, with all the trimmings!

When the war was over, they started the point system, me being the lesser ones, within this setup. They started sending some of those that had been out here the longest, which included my buddy Eddie Foster. It was just that I had been out on another occasion aboard the Chincoteague, but had the privilege of being in the states, while these other units were formed and left the US, some few months ahead of my departure.

I was in a state of panic; Eddie would be leaving in a couple of days and so had most of the galley gang. There was just a skeleton crew left and after Eddie departed, I was really in the dumps. One of my failings, that would haunt me over my life, would be that I was not a good record keeper, never would write down addresses, or contact information. Finally, they closed down operations in the CASU, and I transferred down to Majuro atoll, Eddies, old haunt. I was disappointed, to say the least, for I believed they were sending me home, but this was quite a change in the environment, compared to where I had been; like night and day; there were lots trees and a much cooler climate! Quite a change; nevertheless, this was another unit that was being dismantled and just a hand full of personnel left for the operation, just like me; waiting to go home. I was ready!

Home again, and life move's on!

In 1946, my enlistment was over and the events of WW II slowly faded from my conscious thoughts, so onto the Freeway, of working again, making Babies and slowly the years would pass, one after the other. Slowly, I became a Senior Citizen! One morning, I drove to an automobile dealer's location to have my car serviced. While waiting in line for the doors to open, I began a conversation with the person in front of me; just a casual chat! After a few inquisitive questions, regarding what we had been involved in, I discovered we both had served in the Navy, both in the South Pacific, but then the shocker! Both in the same outfit CASU-F-20.

At this same time, he questioned me regarding this group and their reunions and if I had ever attended any. I had to confess that I had never even contacted one individual that I had been in the service with. He seemed a little puzzled, but that's the way the cookie had crumbled during the years. He had opened a small crack in my distant mind, Eddie Foster! Where are you? This was back in 1983 when the contact information was passed along to me from the fellow I had met at the service line. He had never attended any reunions himself and the contact, I have always felt, was an act of fate!

The following year, I attended this group's reunion in Atlanta, GA, but no Eddie. I scoured their groups list, but to no avail. This would result in an almost two-year search; remember at this time not everyone had a computer, in fact I had not reached that pinnacle of popularity, in most of the public's eyes. Luck, was finally on my side and with the help of someone in the business world I was finally able to locate Eddie, in a small town, west of Chicago and we started corresponding.

Sorry to say I found a stranger. What had happened to the kid I remembered from Roi-Namur? Half of a century of life had passed. Slowly over the months, our friendship returned, but not within the same framework as before. Both of us had been affected by a different tempo of life, older and not just those crazy young boys from another era, but still the friendship came back, just never the same. We both had moved on, changes had affected us, the kids were gone. We were just old seniors now.

We would meet, for the first time, when he and his wife attended the next reunion in Sun-City, AZ. It was quite a shock to see Eddie again. The years had not been kind to him. He had badly injured one of his legs, falling down stairs at a shopping mall. He had disregarded the doctor's advice and had tried walking too soon, resulting in a re- fracturing of the bone in his leg. The result was that he was a physical mess and very bitter about what happened, even though he had caused the problem. We would never see each other again, but would continue to call each other over the next several years.

Eddie was a very talented person with his writing skills and about every month he would send me some of his stories that he had composed. I would save them in a special folder over the years; sadly, Eddie passed away in 2009, from a heart attack. As a tribute to him, I retrieved all the letters he had sent over the years, and composed them into a book format document, sending one to each of his children. I will include the articles that I had saved, and include them in the pages of this book.

"Foster's Journey Friendship"

How do you define friendship! Let me start with the death of a friend, Eddie R. Foster, who lost his struggle to survive in September, of the year 2007. In the last months of 1944 on a small bleak Island in the south pacific during WWII, we became friends.

We came from totally different backgrounds; he was from the south side of Chicago, and I was from a small coastal town in California. Never mind the geography differences, including family structures, but, at 19 years of age we became the best of friends. He was like a brother to me.

Sadly, with the ending of the conflict in 1945 and the disbanding of our Naval Unit, CASU-F-20, we became separated, which at the time was a very emotional jolt to me and even more so, over the years. Sorry to say, but I was not a person to save personal addresses and contact information.

Time, and the years, flew by and those memories were left in the recesses of my mind. Then, due to a casual encounter one day in the late 1980's, at an automotive dealership in California, while engaged in a conversation with an individual waiting for service, we discovered that, during the war, we both had belonged to the same Navy Military Unit and this Unit continued to gather at different times every year for reunions, to exchange stories, along with experiences that had happened during that period of time in their life.

Well to make a long story short, I contacted this reunion group, and attended their next reunion. This prompted a frantic search for my long lost friend. After a search that lasted the better part of a year, we were reunited again, in the mid-1990's, at a reunion in Arizona. It would be the only time we would meet in person.

Over the years we had continued to remain in touch with each other, either during phone conversations, or with letters to each other and over the following years, he sent me many stories and documents that he has written or composed. I have kept them in a file and was very impressed by his ability to express himself in his own unique way, but sadly, he was not able to accomplish his dream of writing a book before his death. So as a tribute to the memory of our friendship and as a compliment to what I believed was a unique talent, I will endeavor to finish this task for my friend, Eddie Foster!

Bill Armstrong!

"Anchor's Away, "Eddie's Journal"

We had a Navy Outhouse called a "Head" in Navy lingo, about 100 yards from the mess hall and from our Quonset hut on Roi. It was not pleasant to visit on a 90-degree day, but it was necessary. It was long overdue to be replaced.

There was not a single female on all of Roi, so to make thing easier for the men; pipes were driven into the ground with funnels stuck into the pipe. This was used to answer nature's call. Eleanor Roosevelt, one of my favorite people, visited the island and we were told not to use the outhouses or funnels until she left. Because she was going to be there all day, the order was ignored.

Eleanor was driven around the island and caught several young men answering nature's call. She talked terrible about us, so two cans of beer a day were taken away. They should not have issued the beer two days, before she came, and there would have been less of a need for the outside facilities.

On Roi, Jackie Cooper (the child actor) entertained troops on both the ships, in the harbor, and for the men on the island. Jackie was a Navy enlisted man with a bad stomach, who could not eat Navy food. He ended each night in the bakeshop eating hot bread crusts, butter and canned peaches. He would entertain the cooks and bakers, by telling us all about Hollywood girls.

Jackie was a great guy. He played drums and told corny jokes in a one-man show. We missed him when he left. Patty Thomas, the then the well-known dancer was another one, who was a class act.

"Eddie the Ship's Baker and His Roi Namur Christmas"

I think it would be best to establish the fact, before any story is told, that of the many Navy men and Marines that were on Roi in 1944, 99% were not there by choice. Roi was not the tropical paradise that it later became.

It was hot, humid, boring—and worse of all; it was several thousand miles from home and girls! You have to remember that 99% of the men were between 17 and 21 years of age. That 1% was an officer, who never had it so good. They had better food, someone to clean up after them, the best living quarters and last, but not least they had all the beer and hard liquor they wanted to buy. Enlisted men were sold two warm cans of beer, six days a week or whenever beer was available.

Now that I've got that point cleared, I will say that most every officer worked hard to make 1944 a good one. Officers and Chiefs were on supply ships every day, trying to get fresh supplies.

Being a baker, my Christmas started a week before December 25th. We started baking the Navy-Aged-Fruit Cake. The only problem was we just had a week to age that which was supposed to age a year…I don't remember that bothering me much, because I had spent four Christmases in the Navy and had never seen anyone eat a piece of fruit cake.

Three days before Christmas, we started baking cherry and apple pies. The ice cream-making machine had been installed in the bakeshop and was going 12 hours a day, storing up ice cream in the freezers. The day before Christmas, we baked mince and pumpkin pies. Everyone was to be served all they could eat of everything.

Christmas dinner was to be served 2P.M. and supper at 7:00 P.M. On the menu, there was turkey, chicken, ham, mashed potatoes, boiled and baked yams, sweet potatoes, creamed carrots, string beans, cabbage slaw, lettuce salad, cranberries, hot rolls, biscuits, cocoa, hot tea, coffee and Pepsi Cola. I watched men eat for two hours!

After the meal, the Chaplains and their assistants stood at the door shaking hands and giving each man a paper bag which contained cigarettes, candy, tooth paste, gum, razor blades, needles, thread, and last, but not least, four Hershey candy bars, that had not turned white yet.

We were privileged to have Patti Thomas, the dancer, and her USO troop who put on four two-hour shows, starting at 4 P.M. until midnight. After their last show, Patti and three of her girls went to the enlisted men's mess hall at midnight, where they were served a dinner consisting of whatever cook and baker thought was their specialty. Being in love with Patti, after seeing her show in the islands several times, I will have to say that those few hours were the highlight of my Navy years.

After having worked 80 or 90 hours in the Christmas week, I'll admit I felt good about it all. I never wanted to do it again--but once was fine. That was a Christmas on Roi as I remember it.

Remembering Fred

Fred A. Hansen

Eddie continues:

For two-and-a-half years Fred was a large part of my life, along with Joe Caldwell and Bill Armstrong. I met Joe and Fred at a Naval Base in Modesto, California, in 1943. Bill Armstrong joined us a few months later. Bill, Fred and I were just on the verge of turning eighteen. Joe was thirty and already had kids of his own.

We were tall for those days. Each of us was close to six feet tall. We were also skinny. None of us would have registered at 130 on a scale, except for Joe. Being tall, skinny and a little feisty were the only ways Fred and I were alike. I always wondered how Fred and I became close friends. To be honest, it was hard to be friends with Fred. He was moody, serious, intense, and hated authority with a passion. This not only kept him in hot water, but also dragged the ones he worked with into it with him. On the plus side, if he was your friend he would lie, cheat, and fight for you. I often thought that he would die for you, if it ever came up.

For those of you, who never knew Fred, let me skip ahead and tell you that he was a member of CASU 20 on Roi, CASU 30 on Majuro, and CASU 17 on Apemama in the Gilbert's. (CASU is Carrier Aircraft Service Unit.) After his discharge from the Navy in 1946, Fred headed for Hollywood, where he became a dancer, choreographer, actor, and show producer.

Fred danced in dozens of musicals, including "Oklahoma" and "Can-Can." He danced in shows such as the Ed Sullivan Show and worked with Juliet Prowse, Frank

Sinatra, Bing Crosby, Milton Berle and many more. Fred produced all of Frank Sinatra's shows at their Nevada casino, just before he died; Fred donated most of his show business collection to the Academy of Dance. That collection included over one hundred autographed pictures from every top name in music and television. He had autographs from Juliet Prowse, Janis Paige, Dean Martin, Jerry Lewis, Marylyn Monroe, Mae West, Shelly Winters, Bing Crosby, Ray Bolger, Marge and Gower Champion, Gale Storm, Lena Horne, and Nat King Cole, just to name a few.

While he served in CASU 20, Fred was a baker. This was a job he hated. He was very vocal about that hate! Fred hated to take an order from anyone. He was smart enough not to argue with Officers or Chief's, but anyone under the rank of Chief would get an argument from Fred anytime they told him what to do.

Fred never mentioned to any of us that he was a full- blooded American Indian, who was adopted off a reservation at the age of five. I learned that from his adoptive mother after WW 11. Fred never spoke of his childhood to any of us, and I would not venture an opinion as to why? Fred and I were both gamblers. Neither of us were very good card players, but I at least, was a lucky dice player. Fred had no luck and was always broke a few hours after payday. We had a lot of time to kill on Roi and we did it by talking. Fred and Joe were not very talkative, so Bill and I did most of the talking. Fred just bitched. We also spent a lot of time in the water behind our quarters where Fred and I shot our 45's that we had liberated from a loading dock on Majuro.

Fred and I were the last of the commissary department to go home. We were put on a Dutch troopship that was undertow. It took us forty days to get back to Los Angeles. We parted there, never to see each other again. We wrote a few times and Bill Armstrong kept in touch with Fred. His last years didn't seem to go very well. His health kept him in the hospital a lot.

I am glad that I had a chance to be friends with those three guys. All three were good friends. Fred lived the most interesting life. Reading through all of the papers that I have been sent over the years has led me to believe that they weren't as happy as they were interesting.

Fred A. Hansen, during rehearsal at the New Frontier Hotel Las Vegas NV, in the1950's

Would I, Eddie, want to go back to Roi?

"I shall return."

A very famous man spoke those famous words and they also had to do with an island. It was a much larger island, but an island nonetheless. It will be 60 years this coming February since the US Navy and Marines arrived in the Marshall Islands, and during those 60 years I was married and raised four children, who supplied me with eight grandchildren and one great-grandson.

I worked hard and had a normal family life. I played every game that used a ball, and was a fishing nut; All in all, it was a pretty good life, except for working in the Chicago winters.

I have been asked several times, during those years by family and friends, if I ever had a desire to return to the Marshalls or Gilberts. My answer was a loud "NO! "Time passed—and arthritis, a broken leg that wouldn't heal, (along with old age) confined me to a wheelchair. Now, I had time to think…

I started to mentally live in the past and part of that past was the Navy and the islands. After Chicago's bitter winters, hot didn't seem so bad. In fact, it started to seem like I had wasted a lot of years freezing, instead of burning.

I always liked the weather in the islands, until it came to trying to sleep in the daytime after working all night. At night there was almost always a breeze off the ocean that made working in the bakeshop almost bearable. Now I began to change my mind. Yeah, I would like to go back.

I would like to visit Majuro, Roi and Eniwetok and have the plane arrive during the afternoon rain. I would like to be there when the rain stopped and see if it was as I remembered it; the air washed clean and sweet, the sky that beautiful blue. I want to look out at blue green water and walk through the clean white sand, as I had done so many times all those years ago.

Most of all, I want to see the changes. When I was there in 1944 and 1945, all the occupied atolls consisted of coral, sand, tents, trucks, planes and men. Now there are stores, shops, bars, restaurants and females. I would like to walk the streets and just marvel at the changes. I would like to find a Marshall Island native, man or woman, who lived during those years I was there and ask about how life was under Japanese rule. Was it better under our occupation?

I would ask how they their living was before World War II and how they make a living now. I would like to ask about their customs and their religion.

As an enlisted man, we were never allowed contact with the Marshallese people, so it would be new to me. I would like to watch the teenagers, to see if there were any differences from those in the states.

Then, I would like to talk to some American servicemen or women and ask about how serving in the Marshalls is now. I'd ask about their quarters, their food and are their officers as chicken as ours were. To this day, 60 years later, I will still say that in three and a half years in the Navy, I only met one officer that I would live next door to.

Then, I would like to sleep one more night there, where it was air conditioned and see if I woke up feeling different than I did 60 years ago.

Last, but not least, I would like to sit in a bar, order a drink and make a toast to all the guys who served with me, then another one to all those who are no longer with us.

After a few of those toasts, this non-drinking old man wouldn't care if his room was air conditioned or not!

Then, I would get back on the plane, ready to go back and resume my life with my family, but yeah---I would love to be like General Mac and return once more.

"Kwajalein- Roi-Namur- Next to Heaven"?

I always read that different people who write of Kwaj.and Roi as being "Next to Heaven and I'm sure they mean just what those words imply, but I'm sure that if you would interview the Navy and Marines who served there in 1944-1945, they would not compare their time on the "Rocks" as "Next to Heaven," but nearer to a place which also starts with H and ends with two Ls.

I was blessed with a good memory and I remember those many years ago when the troopship I was on, arrived in the harbor at Roi-Namur that I, along with about 1,000 other Navy men, stood at the rail and looked at what appeared to be the most God forsaken piece of land in the entire world. It looked like a fairly small chunk of rock with not a bush, tree or blade of grass on the entire island.

When I went down the rope ladder into a small boat and landed on the hot sand, I found I was wrong. There was a tree. One beat-up palm tree that looked like it had taken a direct hit from one of the thousands of bombs and shells Roi had taken. The tree was right next to the one-lane road that connected Roi to Namur.

The first thing I became aware of on Roi was that it was hot and about as humid as it was hot. I also became aware that heat causes thirst, which was quenched with water that was hung from poles in sheepskin bags. The water was so warm; it would have been better used to shower with.

I soon found that the biggest problem was getting through each humid day and night so you could rise early in the morning to start another hot, humid day! Let's remember this took place in 1944 and 1945, when there was no air conditioning and a fan was unheard of. Those of us who worked nights had to sleep in canvas tents during the day and later on we had screened-in Quonset huts.

Our worst enemy was boredom. We had no recreation to speak of. We were not allowed in the water, except in a couple of designated swimming areas. We tried baseball, football and a little basketball, but were taught the hard way that a fall on the combination of sand and coral was hard on the skin and the bones.

Our time was spent in the time-honored Navy way. Griping, bitching and complaining. When we did that long enough, we played dice, cards and Ping-Pong. We sat in the Mess Hall and drank coffee in between griping and complaining. Once in a while something new and different would happen--- like the time the 2nd class cooks got caught behind the blockhouse, marking a new deck of cards that he intended to bring into the poker games, where he was a steady winner. The two guys who caught him were regular donors in the game, so they upped their muscles a little by thumping him in the area of the head!

When he told the story around the gamblers, all his shipmates quit speaking to him, because most of the guys had contributed to his winnings. A couple of weeks later, they found him hanging from the ceiling of the screened-in head. He was cut down in time to save his life and was shipped to Hawaii where he recovered.

Another diversion was one of the cook strikers, who got a "Dear John" letter from his girlfriend and decided the best way to handle that was to take his trusty carbine and threaten to shoot anyone who came in the Quonset hut. One of his friends talked him out of that idea, and he too, was shipped to Hawaii. There were a lot of us who sat down and tried to figure out a scheme that would get us shipped there, but even our fertile minds couldn't come up with anything that would work.

We also had a Marine who was shipped in from a long tour at Guadalcanal; he shot up the movie screen to help Errol kill a few Japanese he was fighting in the movie. He too, was shipped out; only for him they bypassed Hawaii and sent him to Great Lakes to a hospital where they had padding on the walls!

Oh, there were good times. Like the touring major league ball players who came in every couple of months and played a game against each other and then played three innings against a team from the island. My fondest memory of all the years I played every kind of ball was getting a single while hitting against the great, at that time, Ace Adams, who was the major League's first real relief pitcher. He might have cut his 95mph pitch down to 50, but I was still on first base. For an 18-year old boy, that was a real thrill! I got a new ball, signed by all the players and sent it home-then, my ten-year old brother took it out and played ball with it!

Another pleasant memory is the USO and all the nice people who would entertain us. The three I remember best are Bob Hope, the dancer Patti Thomas and the fellow Navy man, Jackie Cooper, who spent a month on Roi entertaining the men on the island and the ships in the harbor. He played good drums and told bad jokes. Most of the entertainers used the mess hall to unwind, after the last shows on board the many big ships, and I got to know both of them quite well.

Jackie had a bad stomach and could not eat Navy food. He would to take a hot loaf of bread, just out of the oven, remove the insides and eat just the crust, covered with a lot of butter. Patti Thomas didn't look to be over 100 pounds and looked even more beautiful to us than she really was. That gal was really special!

All in all it wasn't the place I would have picked to be, but under other conditions, I think I could have learned to like the weather. After a lifetime of the terrible Chicago weather, Roi's hot, humid weather began to appeal to me. I also met and became good friends with a lot of nice guy's, who after 57 years I still remember with love.

So I will continue to read about "Next to Heaven," and still place it close to another place…. but each time I read it, I'll believe it a little more! I do know I'll take tropical to freezing every time!

"We were there, by Bill Armstrong and Eddie Foster"

We came from everywhere; some from Modesto, California, some from Treasure Island, some from the Gilbert Islands and from ships at sea. Men from every state in the Union were to meet at the Barbers Point, Hawaii. Our first destination was to be the Marshall Islands, some to Kwajalein, some to Roi and others to Majuro. We all had one thing in common; we didn't want to be there. Most of us were 17 to 25 years of age and we didn't want to spend our Navy time on a tropical island, even if the native girls wore grass skirts and were topless. We all wanted to go aboard a ship, fighting other ships and going back to civilization to reload and rest.

The Navy had other ideas. They put us on Kwajalein, Roi Namur and later on, Eniwetok, to be subjected to the two B's; bombing, and boredom. Bombing was better. At least it got your blood flowing and gave us something to talk about, besides girls and food.

All of us had left families; Girls, friends, and wives. We missed them. Now our families were either lonely, or without homesick young men. We shared food, water, letters and pictures. We heard grown men sob, when speaking of people we left behind. Some of us were too young to even be out of high school and that created strong lasting friendships. Boys and men from Georgia became fast friends with others from California. Men, who had never seen an ocean before they sailed on one, became friends with guys who lived their whole life in New York, Florida, or California.

There were guys who needed alcohol, in order to cope, and it didn't take long until joy juice was fermenting all over the islands. There were gamblers who killed time with cards and dice. Athletes who played ball and swam, but we all had talking in common and many hours each day were spent, discussing our plans for after the war.

"1995-Fifty Years Later"

I was happy to hear from Bill Armstrong recently. Bill was a shipmate in C.A.S.U- 20 ON Roi-Namur. We were the best of friends, while there. Because I was in a hurry to leave, when my opportunity came, we did not exchange home addresses. Life then became very hectic with raising five kids and we lost track of each other. It was such a nice surprise to hear his voice on the telephone after fifty years.

If you will all bear with me I would like to give you glimpses of the memories I have about my life on Roi-Namur, and Majuro.I remember the Jap pillbox behind our Quonset hut and how we used the hand grenades stored there, to fish with. I think we were hoping to get caught and sent back to the U.S. to be punished...I remember how this sailor, barely eighteen years old, would walk the beach at sun up, looking for seashells. He was so homesick that it wouldn't have taken much to convince him to start swimming back to the U.S.... How time crawled by so slowly that it took a year for a week to go by.... waiting for mail call and to see my shipmates' faces light up when they received mail.... to see the sad looks on faces of those who didn't get any.... I remember the packages I would receive and how almost nothing would be usable, after being on board a supply ship for three or four months.... I remember the coconut cake my sweet old grandmother sent me; in order to use it, I would have to soak it in saltwater for a week, then slice it with a power saw....

I remember during the cigarette shortage in the U.S. People stood in line for hours to buy cigarettes to send to us, when we could buy all we wanted, for five cents a pack.... How I would lie on my stomach for hours and watch the beautiful tropical fish swim by in the little inlet I discovered.... I remember when the jelly fish would come in with the tide and keep all of us from swimming for a couple of days...

How, during the monsoon season, the driving rain would hurt as it hit your face and how we would go outside, during the fresh rains and get a fresh water shower.... How, during the storms, we would have to chain the planes down to keep them from blowing away.... How the temperature would drop eight or ten degrees and some of the guys would shiver, even though it was probably still in the 90's.... How, fifteen minutes after the rain stopped the sun would come out and it looked like it hadn't rained in a year.

Everything looked and smelled so pretty; never was a sky so blue.... How, no one mentioned what could have happened had the tides of war turned and the Japs had come back. They could have taken those rocks back just like we took them. I'm sure we could have given them a hard time, but those rocks would have been hard to defend.... Now to be honest, none of us wanted to be there, but we made the best of it...I remember the endless card games, after payday that went on twenty-four hours a day. Somehow the money always ended up in the hands of the same few every two weeks.... How the CB's got away with things that the sailors would go to the brig for and how they would have liquor brewing in all the barracks, and the parties they would have! I remember the movies we would trade for, with the ships in the harbor. We'd always get the worst of the trade…. I remember the U.S.O. shows that seemed to follow me from island to island, and how I appreciated it then.

The girls looked very well, after looking at ugly men, month, after month…I remember seeing Patty Thomas so often that she seemed like one of my shipmates…. I remember Bob Hope. I never did think he was very funny, but what a wonderful human being!!

How, everyone had a calendar and marked off each day. I don't know how we did it. We had no idea of when we were going home…. I remember looking forward to the island newspaper to find out how the war was going, even though we never got good news…I remember the little bits of sports available and how we watched, just to kill time. I would fly in planes, being tested and put someone else's flight time in for them, so they could get flight pay… How, guys who didn't drink could have the hottest item on the island with his unused beer chit. You could trade for almost anything on the island.

I remember how most guy's never had any racial or ethnic prejudices. My best friends on the island were a black kid from the ghetto in New York, an American Indian from the Menomonee Indian Reservation in Wisconsin, and a white kid from California. Nobody tried to convince me I was wrong in my selection of friends until years later…

Most of all, I remember when the war ended and the Army point system came out. I was so sure I was going home soon that I started packing. Then the Navy came out with their own version and I was sure that being just nineteen and unmarried, I wouldn't get out until the year 2,000. Then the guys begin being discharged.

Fred Hansen and I were the only ones left out of the original commissary division. Fred and I caught the new Executive Officer, making his rounds, and explained to him how long we had been there and how we knew every sand crab and jelly fish by their first name. He told us he would look into it, and much to our surprise, he did.

He came back the next day and said we were right, but there was no one available, in our rating, to take over our jobs. We had a great bunch of guys working with us and some of them stepped up to say that they could take over our jobs, because we really didn't do any work anyway. I still owe Bill Armstrong for that. Bill walked Fred and me out to board the ship that would take us home via the Gilbert Islands. I can still see the sad look on Bills' face, as he walked away.

What I have wanted to say, since I began writing this, is that it was a miserable experience and two wasted years, but I shared it with a great bunch of guys. I know that

I would never want my grandchildren to live it. I do want to attend the next reunion, and sit around with a lot of nice guys and lie about how great it was. It wasn't great, it wasn't pleasant; but it was something that had to be done and I think we did a good job. God willing and if this beaten up old body will give me some help, I'll see most of you guys in Arizona next October. Now there are two questions I would like to ask all of you after all the talking we do. What was the second thing you did when you arrived home!

Eddie Foster   Former Ships Baker   C.A.S.U. 20 AND C.A.S.U. 30

Eddie Foster-Fred Hansen-Roi Island Kwajalein Atoll 1944

www.ingramcontent.com/pod-product-compliance
Lightning Source LLC
Chambersburg PA
CBHW080250290526
45790CB00005B/1763